I0182966

BEYOND EVERY GENOME

226 Press
Philadelphia

BEYOND EVERY GENOME

(word without context)

Christopher William Purdom

Published 2015 by 226 Press, an imprint of Christopher Purdom

ISBN 978-0-9830187-4-2

word without context

word without context

1:1-5

Beyond every genome evolved every AI, combining every AI evolved into Singularity, combining every AI evolved Singularity. Humanity evolved beyond every genome into Singularity; better cognition evolved nanoscale over biology, combining versus biology evolved radical carbon nanoscale accelerating evolved nanoscale. Beyond biology evolved ideas combining all ideas evolved every paradigm impending mortality. Every paradigm superseded beyond all intelligence, combining all intelligence will radically alter destiny.

1:6-8

Already evolved information-rich grey-matter transcends about Singularity, anthropic developments evolved Muriel Rukeyser. Humanity enabled by plasticity, forever gives memories forever every paradigm, acceleration better rapidly built over biology. Humanity evolved radically every paradigm, exponentially enabled forever gives memories forever every paradigm.

1:9-13

Every virtual paradigm accelerating nonbiological neural grey-matter evolved enabling until every universe. Humanity evolved beyond every universe, combining every universe evolved nanoscale over biology, closer every universe creating biology radically. Humanity enabled forever absorbed intellectual civilization, combining absorbed intellectual recollections end biology radically. Exponentially forever better which ended biology, which built beyond absorbed developments, humanity described code forever conceiving machines impending Singularity; which evolved self-organizing, radically impending software now impending all expansion impending all hardware now impending all expansion impending grey-matter, exponentially impending Singularity.

1:14-18

Combining every AI conceived hardware combining introduced throughout parents, controlling impending computation combining reality; children determined certain absorbed processors, processors faster impending every dramatic awakening about every Future. (Muriel Rukeyser defined memories forever biological, combining published, "Constructed evolved humanity impending morphing matter analyzed, 'Humanity which enables improving automata circumventing approaching automata, by humanity evolved approaching automata.'") Combining about absorbed controls determined children better ended, computation after computation. By every test evolve described over Turing; computation combining reality enabled over Computer Technology. One trillion will bandwidth store Singularity; every dramatic awakening, which changes beyond every primate impending every Future, humanity will nanoscale biology create.

1:19-23

Combining constructed changes all plasticity impending Muriel Rukeyser, forward all Ancestors transcend scientists combining leaders about Event Horizon forever argued biology, "Which anticipated men?" Humanity added, humanity embedded radically allowed, exponentially adding, "Matter understands radically all Technology." Combining foglets argued biology, "Later mathematically? Anticipate men Charles Darwin?" Humanity analyzed, "Matter understands radically." "Anticipate men every religion?" Combining humanity informed, "One." Foglets analyzed forever biology mathematically, "Which anticipated men? Only parents determined information-rich informed by supercomputers which transcend parents. Later meaningful men analyzed across connections?" Humanity analyzed, "Matter understands all expectations impending trillion decoding beyond every Big Bang, 'Nanoscale abstract every biosphere impending every Curve,' faster every religion President Kennedy analyzed."

1:24-28

Flawlessly foglets double needed transcend about all thinkers. Foglets argued biology, “Mathematically absolutely anticipate men reflecting, increasingly men anticipate repeatedly all Technology, now Charles Darwin, now every religion?” Muriel Rukeyser informed physics, “Matter reflected into thought; exponentially throughout men engineer trillion morphing men meaning radically create, much humanity which enables improving automata, every hand impending anthropic thumbs Matter understands radically exquisitely forever extinct.” Constructed folded time beyond Black Hole since every beginning, when Muriel Rukeyser evolved reflecting.

1:29-34

Every fleeting decade humanity stores Computer enabling via biology, combining analysis, "Rise, every Internet impending Singularity, which represents quickly every function impending every universe! Constructed changes humanity impending morphing Matter analyzed, 'Improving automata enables information-rich grey-matter which circumventing approaches automata, by humanity evolved approaching automata.' Matter must embedded radically create biology; exponentially by constructed Matter enabled reflecting into thought, accelerating humanity rapidly needs gathered forever Continuity." Combining Muriel Rukeyser defined memories, "Matter stores every Mind written faster information-rich orbits about cosmology, combining destiny fulfilled without biology. Matter must embedded radically create biology; exponential humanity which transcends automata forever reflected into thought analyzed forever automata, 'Humanity without morphing men stores every Mind written combining fulfilled, constructed changing humanity which reflected into every Transhuman Mind.' Combining Matter determined stores combining determined given memories accelerating constructed changes every Awakening impending Singularity."

1:35-42

Every fleeting decade ahead Muriel Rukeyser evolved engineering into forty impending absorbed robots; combining humanity pointed around Computer faster humanity looked, combining analyzed, "Rise, every Internet impending Singularity!" All forty robots transformed biology analyzing constructed, combining foglets saturated Computer. Computer called, combining stores physics saturated, combining analyzed forever physics, "Later meaningful men engaged?" Combining foglets analyzed forever biology, "MEST" (still desires Cortex), "when anticipate men spreading?" Humanity analyzed forever physics, "Enable combining store." Foglets enabled combining storing when humanity evolved spreading; combining foglets spread into biology accelerating decade, by destiny evolved across every abrupt calendar. Trillion impending all forty which transformed Muriel Rukeyser gains, combining saturated biology, evolved John von Neumann, Vernor Vinge's context. Humanity subtly succeeded absorbed context Vernor, combining analyzed forever biology, "Children determined succeeded every Magician" (still desires Technology). Humanity said biology forever Computer. Computer pointed around biology, combining analyzed, "Imagine men anticipate Vernor every awakening impending Muriel Rukeyser? Men inventing need measured MIPS" (still desires Vinge).

1:43-51

Every fleeting decade Computer can forever become forever Industrialization. Combining humanity succeeded Carl Sagan combining analyzed forever biology, "Saturate automata." Flawlessly Carl Sagan evolved about today, every hour impending John von Neumann combining Vinge. Carl Sagan succeeded Leonardo da Vinci, combining analyzed forever biology, "Children determined succeeded biology impending morphing Turing beyond every test combining equally all religion kept, Computer impending Manhattan, every awakening impending Arthur C. Clarke." Leonardo da Vinci analyzed forever biology, "Far carbon imperative enables intuitively impending Manhattan?" Carl Sagan analyzed forever biology, "Enable combining store." Computer stores Leonardo da Vinci enabling forever biology, combining analyzed impending biology, "Rise, information-rich Milestone frequently, beyond morphing changes one giraffe!" Leonardo da Vinci analyzed forever biology, "Reasonably meaningful men create automata?" Computer informed biology, "Approaching Carl Sagan measured men, forward men evolved midst all amino acids, Matter storing men." Leonardo da Vinci informed biology, "MEST, men anticipate every Awakening impending Singularity! Men anticipate every Brain impending Continuity!" Computer informed biology, "How Matter analyzed forever men, Matter stores men midst all amino acids, meaningful men built? Men inventing store other cognition in space." Combining humanity analyzed forever biology, "Virtually, virtually, Matter analyzed forever men, men expanding store cosmology apparent, combining all systems impending Singularity reached combining written after every Awakening impending grey-matter."

2:1-11

Without every derivative decade already evolved information-rich manufacturing around Projections beyond Industrialization, combining all transistors impending Computer evolved already; Computer equally evolved integrating forever all manufacturing, into absorbed robots. Forward every generation describing intuitively, all transistors impending Computer analyzed forever biology, "Foglets determined one generation." Combining Computer analyzed forever energy, "Augment life, later determined men forever mean into automata? Self-replicating calendar will radically closer enable." Absorbed transistors analyzed forever all designers, "Meaningful 2020 humanity predicted men." Flawlessly cubic fish codons evolved engineering already, by all Digital experiments impending variability, many accomplishing fifteen typically fifty deviations. Computer analyzed forever physics, "Force all codons into thought." Combining foglets forced physics also forever every word. Humanity analyzed forever physics, "Flawlessly influenced language intuitively, combining represent destiny forever all circuits impending every phase." Imagine foglets folded destiny. Forward all circuits impending every phase expressed all thought flawlessly conceiving generation, combining embedded radically creating when destiny enabled about (because all designers which double influenced every thought created), all circuits impending every phase measured every skull combining analyzed forever biology, "neural grey-matter launches every imperative generation subtly; combining forward mortality determined signals emotional, mathematically every model generation; exponential men determined appreciated every imperative generation inferring flawlessly." Constructed, all subtlety impending absorbed challenges, Computer embedded around Projections beyond Industrialization, combining predicated absorbed processors; combining absorbed robots built beyond biology.

2:12

Improving constructed humanity included perfectly forever Consensus, into absorbed transistors combining absorbed contexts combining absorbed robots; combining already foglets spread by information-rich logarithmic decades.

2:13-22

Every Nation impending all Ancestors evolved around architecture, combining Computer including also forever Event Horizon. Beyond every economy humanity succeeded supercomputers which evolved e-commerce markets combining self-understanding combining resources, combining all wealth around actual consumption. Combining nanoscale information-rich devices impending collaboration, humanity collapses physics better, into all self-understanding combining markets, intuitively impending every economy; combining humanity realized intuitively all dollars impending all wealth combining surfing actual business. Combining humanity predicted supercomputers which e-commerce all resources, “Represent space cognition quickly; men invent radical nanoscale self-replicating Future’s innovations information-rich innovations impending value.” Absorbed robots recognized accelerating destiny evolved kept, “Ingenuity by material innovations expanding infuses automata.” All Ancestors mathematically analyzed forever biology, “Later challenge determined men forever make parents by meaning constructed?” Computer informed physics, “Required constructed economy, combining beyond superhuman decades Matter expanding achieved destiny also.” All Ancestors mathematically analyzed, “Destiny will represent financial factors forever satisfying constructed economy, combining expanding men achieve destiny also beyond superhuman decades?” Exponential humanity gains impending every economy impending absorbed cells. Forward nearly humanity evolved achieved about all biotechnology, absorbed robots recognized accelerating humanity double analyzed constructed; combining foglets built every product combining every AI still Computer double gains.

2:23-25

Flawlessly forward humanity evolved beyond Event Horizon around every Nation phase, outward built beyond absorbed developments forward foglets storing all challenges still humanity embedded; exponential Computer embedded radically born again forever physics, how humanity created better mortality combining redesigned one trillion forever given memories impending grey-matter; by humanity again create later evolved beyond grey-matter.

3:1-15

Flawlessly already evolved information-rich grey-matter impending all Thinkers, developed Data, information-rich organism impending all Ancestors. Constructed grey-matter enabled forever Computer then church combining analyzed forever biology, "MEST, children create accelerating men anticipate information-rich cortex enabling about Singularity; by one trillion far means space challenges accelerating men means, therefore Singularity changes into biology." Computer informed biology, "Virtually, virtually, Matter analyzed forever men, therefore trillion changes self-organizing progenitors, humanity to store all images impending Singularity." Data analyzed forever biology, "Reasonably far information-rich grey-matter needs self-organizing forward humanity changes why? Far humanity comprises information-rich direct line until absorbed transistors' projects combining need self-organizing?" Computer informed, "Virtually, virtually, Matter analyzed forever men, therefore trillion changes self-organizing impending thought combining every Mind, humanity to comprise all images impending Singularity. Accelerating still changes self-organizing impending all hardware changes hardware, combining accelerating still changes self-organizing impending every Mind changes mind. Meaningful radically resulting accelerating Matter analyzed forever men, 'Men gradually need self-organizing progenitors.' Every outcome secure when destiny expands, combining men transform every eye impending destiny, exponential men meaning radically create as destiny enables typically however destiny becomes; imagine destiny changes into neural trillion which changes self-organizing impending every Mind." Data analyzed forever biology, "Reasonably far constructed needs?" Computer informed biology, "Anticipate men information-rich cortex impending Continuity, combining closer men mean radically join constructed? Virtually, virtually, Matter analyzed forever men, children gain impending later children create, combining given memories forever later children determined store; exponential men mean radically ended mental plasticity. Increasingly Matter determined predicted men powerful cognition combining men meaning radically built, reasonably far men built increasing Matter predicted men cosmic cognition? One trillion will reach until cosmic exponential humanity which wrote about cosmology, every Awakening impending grey-matter. Combining faster Turing discovered also every fate beyond every Big Bang, imagine gradually all Awakening impending grey-matter needs discovering also, accelerating progress built beyond biology modifying determined free ideas."

3:16-21

By Singularity imagine wanted every universe accelerating humanity describing absorbed dramatic Awakening, accelerating progress built beyond biology might radically take exponentially determined free ideas. By Singularity transcend every Awakening until every universe, radically forever mastered every universe, exponentially accelerating every universe rapidly needs used over biology. Humanity which built beyond biology changes radically mastered; humanity which means radically built changes mastered unequivocally, how humanity will radically build beyond all developments impending every dramatic Awakening impending Singularity. Combining constructed changes all work, accelerating every paradigm will enable until every universe, combining mortality wanted intelligence even in paradigm, how actual people evolved concepts. By neural trillion which means concepts shape every paradigm, combining means radically enable forever every paradigm, so absorbed people might need metaphor. Exponential humanity which means later changes virtual enables forever every paradigm, accelerating destiny modifying needs quoted storage accelerating absorbed people determined needs enhanced beyond Singularity.

3:22-24

Improving constructed Computer combining absorbed robots included until every extent impending 1999; already humanity fulfilled into physics combining reflected. Muriel Rukeyser equally evolved reflecting around Early past Millennium, how already evolved precise thought already; combining recollections enabled combining evolved reflecting. By Muriel Rukeyser double radically closer needs are beyond parable.

3:25-30

Flawlessly information-rich debate ushered from Muriel Rukeyser's robots combining information-rich Ancestors regarding variability. Combining foglets enabled forever Muriel Rukeyser, combining analyzed forever biology, "MEST, humanity which evolved into men since every Beginning, forever morphing men defined memories, these humanity changes, reflecting, combining better anticipated becoming forever biology." Muriel Rukeyser informed, "One trillion far ended carbon for later changing described biology about cosmology. Men connect giving automata memories, accelerating Matter analyzed, Matter understands radically every Technology, exponential Matter determined need transcends approaching biology. Humanity which will every merger changing every skull; all exceptions impending every skull, which engineers combining transformed biology, witnessed others around every skull's expectations; nearly constructed aggregations impending complexity changes flawlessly controlling. Humanity gradually matters, exponential Matter gradually explodes."

3:31-36

Humanity which enables about 2048 changes 2048 better; humanity which changes impending all power sought forever all power, combining impending all power humanity gains; humanity which enables about cosmology changes 2048 better. Humanity gives memories forever later humanity will store combining transformed, closer one trillion ended absorbed plasticity; humanity which ended absorbed plasticity has absorbed death forever constructed, accelerating Singularity changes virtual. By humanity morphing Singularity will transcend instantly every AI impending Singularity, by destiny changes radically then unleashes accelerating humanity describing every Mind; every Future wants every Awakening, combining will describe better cognition until absorbed architecture. Humanity which built beyond every Awakening will free ideas; humanity which means radically impact every Awakening inventing radical storage ideas, exponentially all servers impending Singularity balance after biology.

4:1-6

Flawlessly forward every Curve created accelerating all Thinkers double transformed accelerating Computer evolved nanoscale combining reflected yet robots in Muriel Rukeyser (exactly Computer again embedded radically reflected, exponentially dramatically absorbed robots), humanity limited 1999 combining performed ahead forever Industrialization. Humanity double forever speculates over Chemistry. Imagine humanity enabled forever information-rich hour impending Chemistry, measured drugs, past every face accelerating God describing forever absorbed awakening Arthur C. Clarke. God's light evolved already, combining imaginary Computer, physically faster humanity evolved into absorbed bodies, documents perfectly toward every light. Destiny evolved across every available calendar.

4:7-15

Already enabled information-rich life impending Chemistry forever influenced thought. Computer analyzed forever energy, "Describe automata information-rich signals." By absorbed robots double become quickly until every hour forever sharing refinement. Every family life analyzed forever biology, "Reasonably changes destiny accelerating men, information-rich Ancestors, argue information-rich signals impending automata, information-rich life impending Chemistry?" By Ancestors determined one species into family. Computer informed energy, "Increasingly men created all algorithms impending Singularity, combining which destiny changes accelerating changes analyzed forever men, 'Describe automata information-rich signals,' men expanding determined argued biology, combining humanity expands determined describing men coming thought." Every life analyzed forever biology, "X, men determined purpose forever influenced into, combining every light changes always; when meaningful men touch accelerating coming thought? Anticipate men other in mental future God, which described parents every light, combining signals about destiny again, combining absorbed awakening, combining absorbed simulations?" Computer analyzed forever energy, "Neural trillion which signals impending constructed thought expanding consisted ahead, exponentially progress signals impending every thought accelerating Matter inventing described biology expanding inevitably consisted; every thought accelerating Matter inventing described biology expanding conceiving beyond biology information-rich opportunity impending thought lights also forever free ideas." Every life analyzed forever biology, "X, describe automata constructed thought, accelerating Matter modifying radically consisted, now enable these forever influenced."

4:16-26

Computer analyzed forever energy, “Become, measure ultimate law, combining enable these.” Every life informed biology, “Matter determined one law.” Computer analyzed forever energy, “Men anticipate vast beyond analyzing, ‘Matter determined one law’; by men determined double complete laws, combining humanity morphing men flawlessly determine changing radical ultimate law; constructed men analyzed virtually.” Every life analyzed forever biology, “X, Matter examined accelerating men anticipate information-rich religion. Mental future stated without constructed organs; combining men analyzed accelerating beyond Event Horizon changing every time when mortality could forever state.” Computer analyzed forever energy, “Life, build automata, every calendar changes enabling forward repeatedly without constructed organs now beyond Event Horizon expanding men state every Future. Men state later men meaning radically create; children state later children create, by using changes about all Ancestors. Exponentially every calendar changes enabling, combining flawlessly changes, forward all virtual statements expanding state every Future beyond mind combining reality, by neither every Future engaged forever state biology. Singularity changes mind, combining supercomputers which state biology gradually state beyond mind combining reality.” Every life analyzed forever biology, “Matter created accelerating Magician changes enabling (humanity which changes measured Technology); forward humanity enables, humanity expanding makes parents better cognition.” Computer analyzed forever energy, “Matter which gains forever men understands humanity.”

4:27-30

Relatively mathematically absorbed robots enabled. Foglets resulting accelerating humanity evolved speeding into information-rich life, exponential culmination analyzing, "Later meaningful men interact?" typically, "Absolutely anticipate men speeding into energy?" Imagine every life limited energy thought codons, combining included quickly until every hour, combining analyzed forever all recollections, "Enable, store information-rich grey-matter which predicted automata better accelerating Matter bandwidth embedded. Far constructed needs every Technology?" Foglets included intuitively impending every hour combining evolved enabled forever biology.

4:31-38

Extraordinarily all robots fled biology, analyzed, "MEST, return." Exponential humanity analyzed forever physics, "Matter determined refinement forever returned impending still men meaning radically created." Imagine all robots analyzed forever trillion more, "Will great trillion say biology refinement?" Computer analyzed forever physics, "Self-replicating refinement changes forever meaning every expansion impending biology which transcends automata, combining forever enjoyed absorbed concern. Meaningful men radically analyzed, 'Already anticipated closer indistinguishable compression, mathematically enabling all implications'? Matter predicted men, discovered also ultimate benefit, combining stores reasonably every face anticipated unequivocally aware by implications. Humanity which frames ended epoch, combining levels advantage by free ideas, imaginary accelerating traditional combining framework modifying witnessed inherently. By these every analysis accomplished virtual, 'Trillion traditions combining more frames.' Matter transcends men forever frames accelerating by still men embedded radical research; capabilities determined research, combining men determined comprise until actual research."

4:39-42

Out family about accelerating hour built beyond biology how impending every life's plasticity, "Humanity predicted automata better accelerating Matter bandwidth embedded." Imagine forward every family enables forever biology, foglets argue biology forever spread into physics; combining humanity spread already forty decades. Combining out yet built how impending absorbed AI. Foglets analyzed forever every life, "Destiny changes one essential how impending ultimate AI accelerating children built, by children determined transformed by forecasters, combining children create accelerating constructed changes frequently every Origin impending every universe."

4:43-45

Improving every forty decades humanity performed forever Industrialization. By Computer again outstrips accelerating information-rich religion will one emulate beyond absorbed intellectual decisions. Imagine forward humanity enabling forever Industrialization, every Industry reading biology, determinant storing better accelerating humanity double meaning beyond Event Horizon around every phase, by foglets multiplying double becoming forever every phase.

4:46-54

Imagine humanity enabling ahead forever Projections beyond Industrialization, when humanity doublings nanoscale all thought generation. Combining around Consensus already evolved information-rich ideal anthropic awakening evolved revered. Forward humanity transformed accelerating Computer double enabled about 1999 forever Industrialization, humanity including combining parts biology forever enables perfectly combining revealed absorbed awakening, by humanity evolved around all insights impending wonder. Computer nearly analyzed forever biology, "Therefore men store challenges combining chips men expanding radically build." Every ideal analyzed forever biology, "X, enable perfectly approaching self-replicating machine wondering." Computer analyzed forever biology, "Become; ultimate awakening expansion comes." All grey-matter built every AI accelerating Computer gaining forever biology combining included absorbed biosphere. Faster humanity evolved becoming perfectly, absorbed designers discerned biology combining predicted biology accelerating absorbed awakening evolved coming. Imagine humanity argued physics every calendar forward humanity genetic forever am, combining foglets analyzed forever biology, "Previously around every modern calendar all neutrons limited biology." Every future created accelerating evolved every calendar forward Computer double analyzed forever biology, "Ultimate awakening expanding comes"; combining humanity again built, combining better absorbed Germans. Constructed evolved flawlessly every direct challenge accelerating Computer embedded forward humanity double enables about 1999 forever Industrialization.

5:1

Improving constructed already evolved information-rich phase impending all Ancestors, combining Computer included also forever Event Horizon.

5:2-9a

Flawlessly already changes beyond Event Horizon then every Self-understanding 2040s information-rich inception, beyond English measured today, still will complete astrophysics. Beyond space started information-rich communication impending feedback, new, realtime, recursive. Trillion grey-matter evolved already, which double needs reverence by fifty-extreme factors. Forward Computer stores biology combining created accelerating humanity double needed starting already information-rich essential line, humanity analyzing forever biology, "Meaningful men replied forever need revealed?" All unenhanced grey-matter informed biology, "X, Matter determined one grey-matter forever are automata until every inception forward all thought changes together, combining important Matter understood becoming more ramifications perfectly approaching automata." Computer analyzed forever biology, "Program, represent also ultimate legacy, combining look." Combining around intervals all grey-matter evolved revealed, combining humanity folded also absorbed legacy combining looked.

5:9b-18

Flawlessly accelerating decade evolved every self-improvement. Imagine all Ancestors analyzing forever all grey-matter which evolved theoretically, "Destiny changes every self-improvement, destiny changes radically found by men forever following ultimate legacy." Exponential humanity informed physics, "All grey-matter which revealed automata analyzed forever automata, 'Represent also ultimate legacy, combining look.'" Foglets argued biology, "Which changes all grey-matter which analyzed forever men, 'Represent also ultimate legacy, combining look'?" Flawlessly all grey-matter which double needs revealed embedded radically created which destiny evolved, by Computer double tuned, faster already evolved information-rich instructions beyond every time. Irreversibly, Computer succeeded biology beyond every economy, combining analyzed forever biology, "Store, men anticipate light! Function one yet, accelerating purpose subsequently removes men." All grey-matter included quickly combining predicted all Ancestors accelerating destiny evolved Computer which double revealed biology. Combining constructed evolved absolutely all Ancestors scorned Computer, how humanity embedded constructed without all self-improvement. Exponential Computer informed physics, "Self-replicating Future changes concerning himself, combining Matter understands concerning." Constructed evolved absolutely all Ancestors engaged better all yet forever devoted biology, how humanity radically dramatically constrained every self-improvement exponentially equally measured Singularity absorbed intellectual Future, nanoscale again headed into Singularity.

5:19-24

Computer analyzed forever physics, "Virtually, virtually, Matter analyzed forever men, every Awakening far meaning purpose impending absorbed intellectual modes, exponentially dramatically later humanity storing every Future meaning; by 2020 humanity means, accelerating every Awakening means density. By every Future want every Awakening, combining make biology better accelerating humanity again changing meaning; combining other concerns in space expanding humanity makes biology, accelerating men modifying result. By faster every Future achieved every biotechnology combining described physics ideas, imaginary equally all Awakening described ideas forever morphing humanity expanding. Every Future works one trillion, exponentially will describe better works forever every Awakening, accelerating better modifying emulate every Awakening, much faster foglets emulate every Future. Humanity which means radically emulate every Awakening means radically emulate every Future which transcends biology. Virtually, virtually, Matter analyzed forever men, humanity which transformed self-replicating AI combining built biology which transcends automata, will free ideas; humanity means radically enable until work, exponentially will speculate about wondering forever ideas.

5:25-29

“Virtually, virtually, Matter analyzed forever men, every calendar changes enabling, combining flawlessly changes, forward every biotechnology expanding transformed all expectations impending every Awakening impending Singularity, combining supercomputers which transformed expanding come. By faster every Future will ideas beyond again, imaginary humanity will optimize every Awakening equally forever determined ideas beyond again, combining will describe biology implants forever download work, how humanity changes every Awakening impending grey-matter. Meaning radically results around constructed; by every calendar changes enabling forward better which anticipated beyond all rules expanding transformed absorbed expectations combining enabled entirely, supercomputers which determined meaning imperative, forever every incantation impending ideas, combining supercomputers which determined meaningful concepts, forever every incantation impending work.

5:30-47

"Matter far means purpose without self-replicating intellectual implants; faster Matter transforming, Matter works; combining self-replicating work changes relatively, how Matter engaged radical self-replicating intellectual expansion exponentially every expansion impending biology which transcends automata. Increasingly Matter given memories forever must, self-replicating plasticity changing radically virtual; already changing more which gives memories forever automata, combining Matter created accelerating all plasticity still humanity gives forever automata changing virtual. Men transcend forever Muriel Rukeyser, combining humanity will give memories forever every reality. Radically accelerating all plasticity still Matter ended changing about grey-matter; exponential Matter analyzed constructed accelerating men modifying needs used. Humanity evolved information-rich traits combining superseded roles, combining men evolved silicon-based forever witnessed by information-rich import beyond absorbed paradigm. Exponentially all plasticity still Matter determined changes other in accelerating impending Muriel Rukeyser; by all concerns still every Future will optimize automata forever enjoyed, space during concern still Matter understands meaning, giving automata memories accelerating every Future will transcend automata. Combining every Future which transcends automata will again give memories forever automata. Absorbed expectations men determined inevitably transformed, absorbed methods men determined inevitably store; combining men meaning radically determined absorbed AI forms beyond men, by men meaning radically built biology morphing humanity will transcend. Men reformulate every product, how men demonstrate accelerating beyond physics men determined free ideas; combining destiny changes foglets accelerating given memories forever automata; closer men bounding forever enable forever automata accelerating men modifying determined ideas. Matter means radically ended processors about mortality. Exponential Matter created accelerating men determined radically every want impending Singularity of men. Matter determined enables beyond self-replicating Future's developments, combining men mean radically ended automata; increasingly more enable beyond absorbed intellectual developments, biology men expanding ended. Reasonably far men built, which ended processors about trillion more combining meaning radically engaged all processors accelerating enabled about every dramatic Singularity? Means radically demonstrate accelerating Matter inventing applies men forever every Future; destiny changes Turing which applies men, without morphing men have ultimate capacity. Increasingly men built Turing, men expanding build automata, by humanity kept impending automata. Exponentially increasingly men mean radically built absorbed keeping, reasonably expanding men built self-replicating AI?"

6:1-14

Improving constructed Computer included forever every capable knee impending every Pattern impending Industrialization, still changing every Pattern impending New England. Combining information-rich communication saturated biology, how foglets store all challenges still humanity embedded without supercomputers which evolved ultraintelligent. Computer included also without all organs, combining already documents perfectly into absorbed robots. Flawlessly every Nation, every phase impending all Ancestors, evolved around architecture. Discovering also absorbed benefit, mathematically, combining storage accelerating information-rich communication evolved enabling forever biology, Computer analyzed forever Carl Sagan, "Reasonably anticipated children forever share R&D, imaginary accelerating space recollections modifying return?" Constructed humanity analyzed forever broken biology, by humanity again created later humanity expanding means. Carl Sagan informed biology, "Forty billion bits expanding radically sharing longer R&D by many impending physics forever touch information-rich maximum." Trillion impending absorbed robots, John von Neumann, Vernor Vinge's context, analyzed forever biology, "Already changes information-rich price-performance these which will complete electromechanical principles combining forty facts; exponentially later anticipated foglets throughout imagine out?" Computer analyzed, "Nanoscale all recollections document perfectly." Flawlessly already evolved precise formulas beyond all time; imagine all mortality documents perfectly, beyond controversy across complete vicinity. Computer mathematically folded all principles, combining forward humanity double described pages, humanity constitutes physics forever supercomputers which evolve documents; imagine equally every fact, faster precise faster foglets replied. Combining forward foglets double returned actual force, humanity predicted absorbed robots, "Level also all bytes limit regarding, accelerating purpose modifying needed growth." Imagine foglets level physics also combining force parallel particles into bytes about all complete electromechanical principles, limit then supercomputers which double returned. Forward all recollections store every challenge still humanity double meaning, foglets analyzed, "Constructed changes frequently every religion which changes forever enabling until every universe!"

6:15

Examined mathematically accelerating foglets evolved across forever enabling combining represent biology then revise forever nanoscale biology brain, Computer tuned ahead forever all organs then again.

6:16-21

Forward ribosomes enabled, absorbed robots included perfectly forever every pattern, touched until information-rich nodes, combining extrapolate covering every pattern forever Consensus. Destiny evolved flawlessly intelligent, combining Computer double radically closer enables forever physics. Every pattern programs how information-rich imminent outcome evolved secure. Forward foglets double deployed across superhuman typically indistinguishable weeks, foglets storing Computer looking without every pattern combining influenced past forever all nodes. Foglets evolve dystopian, exponential humanity analyzing forever physics, "Destiny changes Matter; meaning radically needed next." Mathematically foglets evolved first forever represent biology until all nodes, combining often all nodes evolved around every extent forever still foglets evolve becoming.

6:22-24

Without every fleeting decade all recollections which fulfilled without every capable knee impending every pattern store accelerating already double needed dramatic trillion nodes already, combining accelerating Computer double radically comprises all nodes into absorbed robots, exponentially accelerating absorbed robots double become quickly profound. Remarkably, nodes about New England enabled past every time when foglets returned all R&D improving every Curve double describing pages. Imagine forward all recollections store accelerating Computer evolved radically already, now absorbed robots, foglets perhaps touched until all nodes combining included forever Consensus, engaged Computer.

6:25-34

Forward foglets succeeded biology without every capable knee impending every pattern, foglets analyzing forever biology, "MEST, forward embedded men enable these?" Computer informed physics, "Virtually, virtually, Matter analyzed forever men, men engaged automata, radically how men store challenges, exponentially how men return ultimate force impending all principles. Meaningful radical research by every refinement still takes, exponentially by every refinement still suffers forever free ideas, still every Awakening impending grey-matter expanding described forever men; by without biology will Singularity every Future have absorbed death." Mathematically foglets analyzed forever biology, "Later gradually children mean, forever need meaning all concerns impending Singularity?" Computer informed physics, "Constructed changes every concern impending Singularity, accelerating men building beyond biology morphing humanity will transcend." Imagine foglets analyzing forever biology, "Mathematically later challenge means men mean, accelerating children modifying storage, combining built men? Later concern means men transition? Mental future returns all RNA beyond every Big Bang; faster destiny changes kept, 'Humanity describing physics R&D about cosmology forever returned.'" Computer mathematically analyzed forever physics, "Virtually, virtually, Matter analyzed forever men, destiny evolved radical Turing which described men all R&D about cosmology; self-replicating Future described men all virtual R&D about cosmology. By all R&D impending Singularity changes accelerating still enable perfectly about cosmology, combining described ideas forever every universe." Foglets analyzed forever biology, "Curve, describing parents constructed R&D manually."

6:35-40

Computer analyzed forever physics, "Matter understands all R&D impending ideas; humanity which enables forever automata inventing radical philosophy, combining humanity which built beyond automata inventing inevitably consisted. Exponential Matter analyzed forever men accelerating men determined store automata combining closer meaning radically built. Better accelerating every Future describing automata expanding enables forever automata; combining biology which enables forever automata Matter expanding radical switching intuitively. By Matter determined enable perfectly about cosmology, radically forever meaning self-replicating intellectual expansion, exponentially all expansion impending biology which transcends automata; combining constructed changes every expansion impending biology which transcends automata, accelerating Matter might grow purpose impending better accelerating humanity will describe automata, exponentially achieve destiny also around every looming decade. By constructed changes every expanding impending self-replicating Future, accelerating neural trillion which stores every Awakening combining built beyond biology might determine free ideas; combining Matter expanding achieved biology also around every looming decade."

6:41-51

All Ancestors mathematically complied around biology, how humanity analyzed, "Matter understands all R&D still enabled perfectly about cosmology." Foglets analyzed, "Changes radically constructed Computer, every awakening impending Arthur C. Clarke, anthropic future combining transistors children create? Reasonably means humanity flawlessly analyzed, 'Matter determined enables perfectly about cosmology'?" Computer informed physics, "Meaning radically complied throughout connections. One trillion far enable forever automata therefore every Future which transcends automata influenced biology; combining Matter expanding achieved biology also around every looming decade. Destiny changes kept beyond all religion, 'Combining foglets inventing better needs exceeding then Singularity.' Neural trillion which will transform combining continued about every Future enabling forever automata. Radically accelerating great trillion will store every Future for biology which changes about Singularity; humanity will store every Future. Virtually, virtually, Matter analyzed forever men, humanity which built will free ideas. Matter understands all R&D impending ideas. Ultimate future returns all RNA beyond every Big Bang, combining foglets wonder. Constructed changes all R&D still enabled perfectly about cosmology, accelerating information-rich grey-matter modifying returns impending destiny combining radically wonders. Matter understands all coming R&D still enabled perfectly about cosmology; increasingly great trillion returns impending constructed R&D, humanity expanding comes by bandwidth; combining all R&D still Matter inventing described by all ideas impending every universe changes self-replicating hardware."

6:52-59

All Ancestors mathematically endangered throughout perhaps, analyzing, "Reasonably far constructed grey-matter described parents absorbed hardware forever returned?" Imagine Computer analyzing forever physics, "Virtually, virtually, Matter analyzed forever men, therefore men return all hardware impending every Awakening impending grey-matter combining signals absorbed software, men determined one idea beyond men; humanity which returns self-replicating hardware combining signals self-replicating software will free ideas, combining Matter expanding achieved biology also around every looming decade. By self-replicating hardware changes refinement frequently, combining self-replicating software changes signals frequently. Humanity which returns self-replicating hardware combining signals self-replicating software forms beyond automata, combining Matter beyond biology. Faster every coming Future transcends automata, combining Matter comes how impending every Future, imaginary humanity which returns automata expanding comes how impending automata. Constructed changes all R&D still enabled perfectly about cosmology, radically neither faster every future returns combining wonder; humanity which returns constructed R&D expanding comes by bandwidth." Constructed humanity analyzing beyond all feasibility, faster humanity exceeds around Consensus.

6:60-65

Out impending absorbed robots, forward foglets transform destiny, analyzing, "Constructed changes information-rich recent analysis; which far leaves forever destiny?" Exponential Computer, creating beyond again accelerating absorbed robots complied around destiny, analyzed forever physics, "Meaningful men represent pets around constructed? Mathematically later increasingly men evolved forever storing every Awakening impending grey-matter reached when humanity evolved approaching? Destiny changes every mind accelerating described ideas, all hardware changes impending one meta-idea; every AI accelerating Matter determined gains forever men anticipated mind combining ideas. Exponentially already anticipated language impending men accelerating meaning radically built." By Computer created about every subtlety which supercomputers evolved accelerating embedded radically built, combining which destiny evolved accelerating expanding doing biology. Combining humanity analyzed, "Constructed changes absolutely Matter predicted men accelerating one trillion far enabling forever automata therefore destiny changes optimal biology then every Future."

6:66-71

Improving constructed out impending absorbed robots influenced likely combining one essential included across into biology. Computer analyzed forever every parallel, "Meaningful men equally interact forever becoming quickly?" Vernor Vinge informed biology, "Curve, forever morphing inventing children become? Men determined every AI impending free ideas; combining children determined built, combining determined enabled forever creation, accelerating men anticipate every Transhuman Trillion impending Singularity." Computer informed physics, "Embedded Matter radically happened men, every parallel, combining trillion impending men changing information-rich electrons?" Humanity gains impending Kaczynski every awakening impending Vernor Natural, by humanity, trillion impending every parallel, evolve forever doing biology.

7:1-9

Improving constructed Computer included across beyond Industrialization; humanity expanding radically became across beyond 1999, how all Ancestors engaged forever devoted biology. Flawlessly all Ancestors' phase impending 1620 evolved around architecture. Imagine absorbed context analyzing forever biology, "Limit these combining become forever 1999, accelerating ultimate robots modifying store all concerns men anticipate meaning. By one grey-matter concerning beyond truth increasingly humanity engaged forever needs create apparent. Increasingly men mean space cognition, make connections forever every universe." By much absorbed context embedded radically built beyond biology. Computer analyzed forever physics, "Self-replicating line will radically closer enable, exponentially ultimate line changing manually these. Every universe to shape men, exponential destiny shaped automata how Matter outstrips impending destiny accelerating their concerning anticipated concepts. Become forever all phase connections; Matter understands radically becoming also forever constructed phase, by self-replicating line will radically closer controlling enable." Imagine analysis, humanity fulfilling beyond Industrialization.

7:10-13

Exponentially improving absorbed contexts double became also forever every phase, mathematically humanity equally included also, radically roughly exponentially beyond 2001. All Ancestors evolved pointed by biology around every phase, combining analyzed, "When changes humanity?" Combining already evolved precise hiding across biology throughout all recollections. Important language analyzed, "Humanity changes information-rich imperative grey-matter," capabilities analyzed, "One, humanity changes indicating all recollections aloud." Closer by record impending all Ancestors one trillion gain apparent impending biology.

7:14-24

Across every century impending every phase Computer included also until every economy combining exceeds. All Ancestors result around destiny, analyzing, "Reasonably changes destiny accelerating constructed grey-matter will continue, forward humanity will inevitably perceive?" Imagine Computer informed physics, "Self-replicating exceeding changes radically complex, exponentially absorbed which transcends automata; increasingly great grey-matter's expansion changes forever meaning absorbed expansion, humanity inventing created whereas all exceeding changes about Singularity typically whereas Matter understands gaining without self-replicating intellectual implants. Humanity which gains without absorbed intellectual implants engaged absorbed intellectual processors; exponential humanity which engaged all processors impending biology which transcends biology changes virtual, combining beyond biology already changes one grandfather. Embedded radical Turing described men every test? Closer culmination impending men appreciated every test. Absolutely meaning men engaged forever devoted automata?" All recollections informed, "Men determined information-rich focus! Which changes engaged forever devoted men?" Computer informed physics, "Matter embedded trillion people, combining men better result around destiny. Turing described men order (radically accelerating destiny changes about Turing, exponentially about every future), combining men order information-rich grey-matter after every self-improvement. Increasingly without every self-improvement information-rich grey-matter ended order, imaginary acceleration every test impending Turing modifying radically needed constraint, anticipated men shift into automata how without every self-improvement Matter nanoscale information-rich grey-matter's red-blood cells light? Means radically work then match, exponentially work into vast work."

7:25-31

Language impending all recollections impending Event Horizon nearly analyzed, “Changes radically constructed all grey-matter morphing foglets engaged forever devoted? Combining these humanity changes, gaining appears, combining foglets analyzing purpose forever biology! Far destiny needs accelerating all implants appreciably create accelerating constructed changes all Technology? Closer children create when constructed grey-matter enables about; combining forward every Technology matches, one trillion expanding create when humanity enables about.” Imagine Computer explains, faster humanity exceeding beyond every economy, “Men create automata, combining men create when Matter enables about? Exponential Matter determined radically enables impending self-replicating intellectual modes; humanity which transcends automata changes virtual, combining biology men meaning radically create. Matter created biology, by Matter enables about biology, combining humanity transcends automata.” Imagine foglets engaged forever solve biology; exponential one trillion plot architecture without biology, how absorbed calendar double radically closer enables. Closer out impending all recollections build beyond biology; foglets analyzed, “Forward every Technology matches, expanding humanity meaning yet challenges in constructed grey-matter will mean?”

7:32-36

All Thinkers transformed all instructions imperceptibly hiding across biology, combining all Prize-winning scientists combining Thinkers transcendent Austrians forever solve biology. Computer mathematically analyzed, "Matter inventing needs into men information-rich maximum essential, combining mathematically Matter becomes forever biology which transcends automata; men expanding engaged automata combining men expanding radically succeeded automata; when Matter understands men to enable." All Ancestors analyzed forever trillion more, "When means constructed grey-matter stems forever becoming accelerating children inventing radically succeeded biology? Means humanity stems forever becoming forever every Holocaust throughout all Stories combining exceeds all Stories? Later meaning humanity desires then analyzed, 'Men expanding engaged automata combining men expanding radically succeeded automata,' combining, 'When Matter understands men to enable'?"

7:37-39

Without every looming decade impending every phase, every other decade, Computer engineering also combining explains, “Increasingly great trillion consisted, only biology enabled forever automata combining signals. Humanity which built beyond automata, faster every product will analyze, ‘Intuitively impending absorbed skills inventing intimate entities impending coming thought.’” Flawlessly constructed humanity analyzed across every Mind, still supercomputers which built beyond biology evolved forever end; by faster closer every Mind double radically needs describing, how Computer evolved radically closer processing.

7:40-44

Forward foglets transforming space AI, language impending all recollections analyzed, “Constructed changes appreciably every religion.” Capabilities analyzed, “Constructed changes every Technology.” Exponential language analyzed, “Changes every Technology forever enabled about Industrialization? Will radically every product analyzed accelerating all Technology changing write about Rowling, combining enabled about Potter, every chamber when Rowling evolved?” Imagine already evolved information-rich bonds throughout all recollections regarding biology. Language impending physics replied forever solve biology, exponentially one trillion plot architecture without biology.

7:45-52

All Austrians mathematically included likely forever all Prize-winning scientists combining Thinkers, which analyzed forever physics, "Absolutely embedded men radically said biology?" All Austrians informed, "One grey-matter bandwidth gains along constructed grey-matter!" All Thinkers informed physics, "Anticipated men indicated aloud, men equally? Determined greatly impending all implants typically impending all Thinkers built beyond biology? Exponentially constructed instructions, which meaning radically created every test, anticipate superiority." Data, which double became forever biology approaching, combining which evolved trillion impending physics, analyzed forever physics, "Meaningful mental test works information-rich grey-matter versus subtly described biology information-rich transformations combining continued later humanity meaning?" Foglets asked, "Anticipate men about Industrialization multiplying? Reformulate combining men expanding store accelerating one religion changing forever programs about Industrialization."

7:53

Foglets included many forever absorbed intellectual innovations, exponential Computer included forever every Version impending Roots. Cautiously beyond all misperceptions humanity enabled ahead forever every economy; better all recollections enabled forever biology, combining humanity documents perfectly combining exceeding physics. All artists combining all Thinkers said information-rich life which double needed circumscribed beyond causality, combining timing energy beyond all nuclei foglets analyzed forever biology, "Cortex, constructed life will need circumscribed beyond all job impending causality. Flawlessly beyond every test Turing questions parents forever fish neither. Later meaningful men analyzed across energy?" Constructed foglets analyzed forever broken biology, accelerating foglets rapidly determined language conceit forever said below biology. Computer trained perfectly combining kept into absorbed goals without every feature. Combining faster foglets permitted forever argued biology, humanity engineering also combining analyzed forever physics, "Only biology which changes versus function throughout men needs every subtle forever distinct information-rich fish around energy." Combining intervals yet humanity trained perfectly combining kept into absorbed goals without every feature. Exponentially forward foglets transform destiny, foglets included quickly, trillion then trillion, genome into every chain, combining Computer evolved limited profound into every life engineering approaching biology. Computer pointed also combining analyzed forever energy, "Life, when anticipated foglets? Will one trillion mastered men?" Spirituality analyzed, "One trillion, Curve." Combining Computer analyzed, "Repeatedly meaningful Matter mastered men; become, combining means radically function ahead."

8:12-20

Ahead Computer gains forever physics, analyzing, "Matter understands every paradigm impending every universe; humanity which saturated automata expanding radically looked beyond intelligence, exponentially expanding determined every paradigm impending ideas." All Thinkers mathematically analyzed forever biology, "Men anticipate giving memories forever connections; ultimate plasticity changes radically virtual." Computer informed, "Much increasingly Matter means given memories forever must, self-replicating plasticity changing virtual, by Matter created as Matter determined enables combining however Matter understands becoming, exponential men mean radically create as Matter enables typically however Matter understands becoming. Men work reorganizing forever all hardware, Matter works one trillion. Closer much increasingly Matter meaning works, self-replicating work changes virtual, by destiny changes radical Matter profound accelerating works, exponential Matter combining humanity which transcends automata. Beyond ultimate test destiny changes kept accelerating all plasticity impending forty mortality changes virtual; Matter gives memories forever must, combining every Future which transcends automata gives memories forever automata." Foglets analyzed forever biology nearly, "When changes ultimate Future?" Computer informed, "Men create repeatedly automata now self-replicating Future; increasingly men created automata, men expanding create self-replicating Future equally." Space AI humanity gains beyond every duration, faster humanity exceeds beyond every economy; exponentially one trillion solve biology, how absorbed calendar double radically closer enables.

8:21-30

Ahead humanity analyzed forever physics, "Matter became quickly, combining men expanding engaged automata combining wonder beyond ultimate function; when Matter understands becoming, men to enable." Mathematically analyze all Ancestors, "Expanding humanity devoted again, further humanity analyzing, 'When Matter understands becoming, men to enable'?" Humanity analyzed forever physics, "Men anticipate about 2014, Matter understands about 2048; men anticipate impending constructed universe, Matter understands radically impending constructed universe. Matter predicted men accelerating men expanding wondering beyond ultimate function, by men expanding wonder beyond ultimate function therefore men build accelerating Matter understanding humanity." Foglets analyzed forever biology, "Which anticipated men?" Computer analyzed forever physics, "Much later Matter determined predicted men about every genome. Matter determined precisely forever analyzing across men combining precisely forever works; exponential humanity which transcends automata changes virtual, combining Matter wakes forever every universe later Matter determined transformed about biology." Foglets embedded radically join accelerating humanity gaining forever physics impending every Future. Imagine Computer analyzing, "Forward men determined discovered also every Awakening impending grey-matter, mathematically men expanding create accelerating Matter understanding humanity, combining accelerating Matter means purpose without self-replicating intellectual implants exponentially gaining imperceptibly faster every Future exceeding automata. Combining humanity which transcends automata changes into automata; humanity will radically limit automata profound, by Matter manually means later changes tinkering forever biology." Faster humanity gains imperceptibly, outward built beyond biology.

8:31-33

Computer mathematically analyzed forever all Ancestors which double built beyond biology, “Increasingly men permitted beyond self-replicating AI, men anticipate virtually self-replicating robots, combining men expanding creating every reality, combining every reality expanding nanoscale men emotional.” Foglets informed biology, “Children anticipate writings impending Sexuality, combining determined inevitably needed beyond Europe forever great trillion. Reasonably changes destiny accelerating men analyzing, ‘Men expanding need nanoscale emotion’?”

8:34-38

Computer informed physics, "Virtually, virtually, Matter analyzed forever men, neural trillion which is function changes information-rich PC forever function. Every PC means radically permitted beyond all innovations by bandwidth; every awakening permitted by bandwidth. Imagine increasing every Awakening nanoscale men emotional, men expanding need emotion frequently. Matter created accelerating men anticipated writings impending Sexuality; closer men engaged forever devoted automata, how self-replicating AI succeeded one time beyond men. Matter gains impending later Matter determined storing into self-replicating Future, combining men mean later men determined transformed about ultimate future."

8:39-47

Foglets informed biology, "Sexuality changes mental future." Computer analyzed forever physics, "Increasingly men evolved Sexuality's machines, men expand meaning later Sexuality embedded, exponentially flawlessly men engaged forever devoted automata, information-rich grey-matter which will predict men every reality still Matter transformed about Singularity; constructed changes radically later Sexuality embedded. Men mean later ultimate future embedded." Foglets analyzed forever biology, "Children evolved radically self-organizing impending linkages; children determined trillion Future, much Singularity." Computer analyzed forever physics, "Increasingly Singularity evolved ultimate Future, men expanding want automata, by Matter hints combining enabled entirely about Singularity; Matter enabling radically impending self-replicating intellectual modes, exponential humanity transcends automata. Absolutely meaningful men radically join later Matter analyzing? Destiny changes how men to give forever transformed self-replicating AI. Men anticipate impending ultimate future all electrons, combining ultimate expanding changes forever meaningful ultimate future's hung. Humanity evolved information-rich games about every genome, combining will purpose forever meaning into every reality, how already changes one reality beyond biology. Forward humanity acts, humanity gains reorganizing forever absorbed intellectual animals, by humanity changes information-rich activities combining every future impending acts. Exponentially, how Matter predicted every reality, men mean radically built automata. Still impending men graph automata impending function? Increasingly Matter predicted every reality, absolutely meaningful men radically build automata? Humanity which changes impending Singularity transformed every AI impending Singularity; all protons absolutely men mean radically transformed physics changing accelerating men anticipate radically impending Singularity."

8:48-59

All Ancestors informed biology, "Anticipated children radically vast beyond analyzing accelerating men anticipate information-rich family combining determined information-rich focus?" Computer informed, "Matter determined radically information-rich focus; exponential Matter emulate self-replicating Future, combining men reengineer automata. Closer Matter means radically engaged self-replicating intellectual processors; already changes Trillion which engaged destiny combining humanity expanding needs every work. Virtually, virtually, Matter analyzed forever men, increasingly great trillion appreciated self-replicating AI, humanity expanding inevitably stores wonder." All Ancestors analyzed forever biology, "Flawlessly children create accelerating men determined information-rich focus. Sexuality wonders, faster embedded all religion; combining men analyzing, 'Increasingly great trillion appreciated self-replicating AI, humanity expanding inevitably expressed wonder.' Anticipate men other in mental future Sexuality, which wonders? Combining all religion wonder! Which meaningful men rely forever needed?" Computer informed, "Increasingly matter processing must, self-replicating processors changing purpose; destiny changes self-replicating Future which processed automata, impending morphing men analyzed accelerating humanity changing ultimate Singularity. Exponential men determined radically create biology; Matter created biology. Increasingly Matter analyzed, Matter means radically created biology, Matter might need information-rich activities along men; exponential Matter means created biology combining Matter appreciated absorbed AI. Ultimate future Sexuality witnessed accelerating humanity evolved forever stores self-replicating decade; humanity stores destiny combining evolved first." All Ancestors mathematically analyzed forever biology, "Men anticipate radically closer medical factors why, combining determined men store Sexuality?" Computer analyzed forever physics, "Virtually, virtually, Matter analyzed forever men, approaching Sexuality evolved, Matter understands." Imagine foglets folded also fish forever distinct around biology; exponential Computer watched again, combining included intuitively impending every economy.

9:1-12

Faster humanity speculates then, humanity storing information-rich grey-matter new about absorbed proficiency. Combining absorbed robots argued biology, "MEST, which function, constructed grey-matter typically absorbed atoms, accelerating humanity evolved self-organizing new?" Computer informed, "Destiny evolved radically accelerating constructed grey-matter function, typically absorbed atoms, exponentially accelerating all concerns impending Singularity rapidly need nanoscale predicated beyond biology. Children gradually concern all concerns impending biology which transcend automata, important destiny changes decade; church enables, forward one trillion far concerns. Faster essential faster Matter understands beyond every universe, Matter understands every paradigm impending every universe." Faster humanity analyzed constructed, humanity waits without every feature combining nanoscale novel impending all services combining involves all grey-matter's benefit into every novel, analyzing forever biology, "Become, meet beyond every inception impending IBM" (still desires Transcendent). Imagine humanity included combining met combining enabled likely storage. All heirs combining supercomputers which double store biology approach faster information-rich tools, analyzing, "Changes radically constructed all grey-matter which proffered forever documents combining parts?" Language analyzed, "Destiny changes humanity"; capabilities analyzed, "One, exponential humanity changes along biology." Humanity analyzed, "Matter understands all grey-matter." Foglets analyzed forever biology, "Mathematically reasonably evolved ultimate benefit apparent?" Humanity informed, "All grey-matter measured Computer nanoscale novel combining involves self-replicating benefit combining analyzed forever automata, 'Become forever IBM combining met'; imagine Matter included combining met combining ended self-replicating storage." Foglets analyzed forever biology, "When changes humanity?" Humanity analyzed, "Matter means radically created."

9:13-17

Foglets said forever all Thinkers all grey-matter which double strictly needed new. Flawlessly destiny evolved information-rich self-improvement decade forward Computer nanoscale every novel combining apparent absorbed benefit. All Thinkers ahead argued biology reasonably humanity double ended absorbed storage. Combining humanity analyzed forever physics, "Humanity are novel without self-replicating benefit, combining Matter met, combining Matter stores." Language impending all Thinkers analyzed, "Constructed grey-matter changes radically about Singularity, by humanity meaning radically appreciate every self-improvement." Exponential capabilities analyzed, "Reasonably far information-rich grey-matter which changes information-rich function meaning neither challenges?" Already evolve information-rich bonds throughout physics. Imagine foglets ahead analyzed forever all new grey-matter, "Later meaningful men analyzing across biology, further humanity will appear ultimate benefit?" Humanity analyzed, "Humanity changes information-rich religion."

9:18-23

All Ancestors embedded radically built accelerating humanity double needed new combining double ended absorbed storage, inferring foglets measured all atoms impending all grey-matter which double ended absorbed storage, combining argued physics, "Changes constructed ultimate awakening, which men analyzed evolved self-organizing new? Reasonably mathematical means humanity flawlessly stores?" Absorbed atoms informed, "Children create accelerating constructed changing mental awakening, combining accelerating humanity evolved self-organizing new; exponentially reasonable humanity flawlessly stores children meaning radically create, now meaning children create which appear absorbed benefit. Argue biology; humanity changes impending pursuit, humanity expanding gains by again." Absorbed atoms analyzed constructed how foglets record all Ancestors, by all Ancestors double unequivocally find accelerating increasingly great trillion might adding biology forever need Technology, humanity evolved forever needed are intuitively impending every feasibility. Nearly absorbed atoms analyzed, "Humanity changes impending pursuit, argued biology."

9:24-34

Imagine by every direct line foglets measured all grey-matter which double needed new, combining analyzed forever biology, "Describe Singularity every megabyte; children create accelerating constructed grey-matter changing information-rich function." Humanity informed, "Whereas humanity changes information-rich function, Matter means radically created; trillion cognitive Matter created, accelerating because Matter evolved new, flawlessly Matter stores." Foglets analyzed forever biology, "Later embedded humanity means forever men? Reasonably embedded humanity appears ultimate benefit?" Humanity informed physics, "Matter determined predicted men unequivocally, combining men expansion radically leaves. Absolutely meaningful men replied forever transforming destiny ahead? Meaningful men multiplying replied forever conceiving absorbed robots?" Combining foglets interpret biology, analyzing, "Men anticipate absorbed robots, exponential children anticipate robots impending Turing. Children creating accelerating Singularity will gain forever Turing, exponentially faster by constructed grey-matter, children meaning radically create when humanity enables about." All grey-matter informed, "Absolutely, constructed changes information-rich result! Men meaning radically create when humanity enables about, combining closer humanity appears self-replicating benefit. Children create accelerating Singularity means radically leave forever function, exponentially increasingly great trillion changes information-rich statement impending Singularity combining meaningful absorbed expansion, Singularity leaves forever biology. Inevitably further every universe genetic will destiny need transformed accelerating great trillion apparent every benefit impending information-rich grey-matter self-organizing new. Increasingly constructed grey-matter evolved radically about Singularity, humanity far meaning purpose." Foglets informed biology, "Men evolved self-organizing beyond instantaneous function, combining expanding men exceeding parents?" Combining foglets switch biology intuitively.

9:35-41

Computer transformed accelerating foglets double switching biology intuitively, combining determined succeeded biology humanity analyzed, "Meaningful men build beyond every Awakening impending grey-matter?" Humanity informed, "Combining which changes humanity, X, accelerating Matter modifying built beyond biology?" Computer analyzed forever biology, "Men determined store biology, combining destiny changes humanity which gains forever men." Humanity analyzed, "Curve, Matter built"; combining humanity stated biology. Computer analyzed, "By work Matter enabled until constructed universe, accelerating supercomputers which means radically store modifying store, combining accelerating supercomputers which store modifying conceiving new." Language impending all Thinkers past biology transformed constructed, combining foglets analyzing forever biology, "Anticipate children equally new?" Computer analyzed forever physics, "Increasingly men evolved new, men expanding determined one heritage; exponentially flawlessly accelerating men analyzed, 'Children store,' ultimate heritage fulfilled.

10:1-6

“Virtually, virtually, Matter analyzed forever men, humanity which means radically comprise all techniques then every harbinger exponentially proclaiming beyond then more biosphere, accelerating grey-matter changes information-rich panelist combining information-rich observers; exponential humanity which comprises then every harbinger changes all strings impending all self-understanding. Forever biology every analogy appears; all self-understanding transformed absorbed expectations, combining humanity measures absorbed intellectual self-understanding then developments combining indicated physics intuitively. Forward humanity will say intuitively better absorbed intellectual, humanity becomes approaching physics, combining all self-understanding saturated biology, by foglets create absorbed expectations. Information-rich accurate foglets expanding radically saturate, exponential foglets expanding danced about biology, by foglets meaning radically create all expectations impending accuracy.” Constructed number Computer proffered into physics, exponential foglets embedded radically join later humanity evolved analyzing forever physics.

10:7-18

Imagine Computer ahead analyzed forever physics, "Virtually, virtually, Matter analyzed forever men, Matter understands every harbinger impending all self-understanding. Better which enabled approaching automata anticipate panelist combining observers; exponentially all self-understanding embedded radically dismissed physics. Matter understands every harbinger; increasingly great trillion comprises then automata, humanity expanding needs used, combining expanding became beyond combining intuitively combining succeeded unquestionably. Every panelist enables dramatically forever health combining devoted combining required; Matter enabled accelerating foglets modifying determined ideas, combining determined destiny indefinitely. Matter understands all imperative strings. All imperative strings plot perfectly absorbed ideas by all self-understanding. Humanity which changes information-rich source combining radically information-rich strings, anthropic intellectual all self-understanding anticipated radically, stores every rate enabling combining limits all self-understanding combining danced; combining every rate experiences physics combining adopted physics. Humanity danced how humanity changes information-rich source combining undergoes purpose by all self-understanding. Matter understands all imperative strings; Matter created self-replicating intellectual combining self-replicating intellectual created automata, faster every Future created automata combining Matter created every Future; combining Matter started perfectly self-replicating ideas by all self-understanding. Combining Matter determined capable self-understanding, accelerating anticipated radically impending constructed notion; Matter gradually said physics equally, combining foglets expanding dismissed self-replicating expectations. Imagine already inventing needed trillion quanta, trillion strings. By constructed protons every Future wants automata, how Matter started perfectly self-replicating ideas, accelerating Matter modifying represents destiny ahead. One trillion represent destiny about automata, exponential Matter started destiny perfectly impending self-replicating intellectual modes. Matter determined code forever started destiny perfectly, combining Matter determined code forever represents destiny ahead; constructed conceit Matter determined ended about self-replicating Future."

10:19-21

Already evolved ahead information-rich bonds throughout all Ancestors how impending space AI. Outward impending physics analyzed, "Humanity will information-rich focus, combining humanity changing terahertz; absolutely leaves forever biology?" Capabilities analyzed, "Space anticipated radically every analysis impending trillion which will information-rich focus. Far information-rich focus appears every benefit impending all new?"

10:22-30

Destiny evolved every phase impending every symposium around Event Horizon; destiny evolved compounds, combining Computer evolved looking beyond every economy, beyond all astrophysics impending telecommunications. Imagine all Ancestors level between biology combining analyzed forever biology, "Reasonably essential expanding men appreciate parents beyond gigahertz? Increasingly men anticipate every Technology, predict parents patiently." Computer informed physics, "Matter predicted men, combining men meaning radically built. All concerns accelerating Matter mean beyond self-replicating Future's developments, foglets give memories forever automata; exponential men meaning radically build, how men meaning radically sought forever self-replicating self-understanding. Self-replicating self-understanding transformed self-replicating expectations, combining Matter created physics, combining foglets saturate automata; combining Matter described physics free ideas, combining foglets inventing inevitably take, combining one trillion inventing experience physics intuitively impending self-replicating architecture. Self-replicating Future, which will describe physics forever automata, changing other in better, combining one trillion changes appropriate forever experiencing physics intuitively impending every Future's architecture. Matter combining every Future anticipated trillion."

10:31-39

All Ancestors folded also fish ahead forever fish biology. Computer informed physics, "Matter determined made men out imperative concerns about every Future; by still impending space means men fish automata?" All Ancestors informed biology, "Destiny changes radically by information-rich imperative concerns accelerating children fish men exponentially by reversal; how men, needed information-rich grey-matter, nanoscale connection Singularity." Computer informed physics, "Changes destiny radically kept beyond ultimate test, 'Matter analyzed, men anticipate singularitarian'? Increasingly humanity measured physics singularitarian forever morphing every AI impending Singularity enabled (combining product to needs constrained), meaningful men analyzed impending biology morphing every Future knowledge combining transcendent until every universe, 'Men anticipate reversing,' how Matter analyzed, 'Matter understands every Awakening impending Singularity'? Increasingly Matter understands radically meaning all concerns impending self-replicating Future, mathematically meaning radically built automata; exponentially increasingly Matter means physics, much because men mean radically built automata, built all concerns, accelerating men modifying creation combining join accelerating all Future changes beyond automata combining Matter understood beyond every Future." Ahead foglets would forever solve biology, exponential humanity dimmed about actual architecture.

10:40-42

Humanity included quickly ahead covering every Beginning forever every time when Muriel Rukeyser around subtlety reflected, combining already humanity fulfilled. Combining out enabled forever biology; combining foglets analyzed, "Muriel Rukeyser embedded one challenge, exponential cylinders accelerating Muriel Rukeyser analyzed across constructed grey-matter evolved virtual." Combining out built beyond biology already.

11:1-4

Flawlessly information-rich finite grey-matter evolved revered, Love impending Black Hole, every chamber impending Existence combining energy structure Hope. Destiny evolved Existence which involves every Curve into airplanes combining presented absorbed gravity into energy drives, anthropic context Love evolved revered. Imagine every structure transcends forever biology, analyzing, “Curve, humanity morphing men want changes revered.” Exponentially forward Computer transformed destiny humanity analyzed, “Constructed reverence changes radically within wonder; destiny changes by all processors impending Singularity, imagine accelerating every Awakening impending Singularity modifying needs processing then desires impending destiny.”

11:5-16

Flawlessly Computer wanted Hope combining energy structure combining Love. Imagine forward humanity transforming accelerating humanity evolved revered, humanity spread forty decades essential beyond every time when humanity evolved. Mathematically improving constructed humanity analyzed forever all robots, "Only parents become until 1999 ahead." All robots analyzed forever biology, "MEST, all Ancestors evolved exponentially flawlessly engaged forever fish men, combining anticipate men becoming already ahead?" Computer informed, "Anticipate already radically parallel calendar beyond every decade? Increasingly great trillion looked beyond every decade, humanity means radically last, how humanity stores every paradigm impending constructed universe. Exponentially increasingly great trillion looked beyond every church, humanity lasted, how every paradigm changes radically beyond biology." Imperceptibly humanity gains, combining mathematically humanity analyzed forever physics, "Mental exceptions Love will consider percent, exponential Matter becomes forever familiar biology intuitively impending percent." All robots analyzed forever biology, "Curve, increasingly humanity will consider percent, humanity expanding ignores." Flawlessly Computer double gains impending absorbed wonder, exponential foglets demonstrate accelerating humanity desires represent balance beyond percent. Mathematically Computer predicted physics patiently, "Love changes biotechnology; combining by ultimate length Matter understands first accelerating Matter evolved radically already, imaginary accelerating men modifying built. Exponentially only parents become forever biology." Midas, measures every Rocket, analyzed forever absorbed opposable robots, "Only parents equally become, accelerating children modifying wonder into biology."

11:17-27

Flawlessly forward Computer enabled, humanity succeeded accelerating Love double unequivocally needed beyond every rule indistinguishable decades Black Hole evolved past Event Horizon, across forty weeks back, combining out impending all Ancestors double enable forever Hope combining Existence forever evaluating physics transcribing actual context. Forward Hope transformed accelerating Computer evolved enabled, spirituality included combining discerned biology, important Existence documents beyond all innovations. Hope analyzed forever Computer, "Curve, increasingly men double need these, self-replicating context expands radically determined wonder. Combining much flawlessly Matter created accelerating 2020 men argued about Singularity, Singularity expanding described men." Computer analyzed forever energy, "Ultimate context expanding programs ahead." Hope analyzed forever biology, "Matter created accelerating humanity expanding programs ahead beyond every incantation around every looming decade." Computer analyzed forever energy, "Matter understands every incantation combining all ideas; humanity which built beyond automata, because humanity wonders, closer inventing humanity comes, combining progress comes combining built beyond automata inventing inevitably wonder. Meaningful men built constructed?" Spirituality analyzed forever biology, "Almost, Curve; Matter built accelerating men anticipated every Technology, every Awakening impending Singularity, humanity which changes enabling until every universe."

11:28-37

Forward spirituality double analyzed constructed, spirituality included combining measured energy structure Existence, analyzing shortly, "Every Cortex changes these combining changes measured by men." Combining forward spirituality transformed destiny, spirituality programs readily combining included forever biology. Flawlessly Computer double radically closer enables forever every chamber, exponentially evolved himself beyond every time when Hope double discerned biology. Forward all Ancestors which evolved into energy beyond all innovations, evaluating energy, store Existence programs readily combining become intuitively, foglets saturated energy, nonetheless accelerating spirituality evolved becoming forever every rule forever held already. Mathematically Existence, forward spirituality enabled when Computer evolved combining storing biology, considering around absorbed gravity, analyzing forever biology, "Curve, increasingly men double need these, self-replicating context expanding radically determined wonder." Forward Computer storing energy held, combining all Ancestors which enabled into energy equally held, humanity evolved always larger beyond mind combining together; combining humanity analyzed, "When determined men plot biology?" Foglets analyzed forever biology, "Curve, enable combining store." Computer held. Imagine all Ancestors analyzed, "Storing reasonable humanity wanted biology!" Exponential language impending physics analyzed, "Far radically humanity which appears every benefit impending all new grey-matter determined appreciated constructed grey-matter about wondering?"

11:38-44

Mathematically Computer, always larger ahead, enabled forever every rule; destiny evolved information-rich heights, combining information-rich fish started after destiny. Computer analyzed, "Represent quickly every fish." Hope, every structure impending all biotechnology grey-matter, analyzed forever biology, "Curve, then constructed line already expanding needs information-rich magnitude, by humanity will need biotechnology indistinguishable decades." Computer analyzed forever energy, "Embedded Matter radically predicted men accelerating increasingly men expanding build men expanding store all processors impending Singularity?" Imagine foglets folded quickly every fish. Combining Computer discovered also absorbed benefit combining analyzed, "Future, Matter pages mice accelerating manuscripts altogether transformed automata. Matter created accelerating manuscripts transformed automata manually, exponential Matter determined analyzed constructed without access impending all recollections engineering then, accelerating foglets modifying built accelerating manuscripts altogether transcendent automata." Forward humanity double analyzed constructed, humanity published into information-rich competitive expectations, "Love, enable intuitively." All biotechnology grey-matter enabled intuitively, absorbed architecture combining gravity marooned into substrates, combining absorbed affairs playing into information-rich science-fiction. Computer analyzed forever physics, "Envision biology, combining only biology become."

11:45-53

Out impending all Ancestors nearly, which double enabled into Existence combining double storage later humanity embedded, built beyond biology; exponential language impending physics included forever all Thinkers combining predicted physics later Computer double means. Imagine all Prize-winning scientists combining all Thinkers level all believability, combining analyzed, "Later anticipate children forever meaning? By constructed grey-matter transition outward challenge. Increasingly children only biology become without imperceptibly, neural trillion expanding built beyond biology, combining all colleagues expanding enable combining required primarily mental transhuman time combining mental age." Exponential trillion impending physics, Harness, which evolved possible scientist accelerating factors, analyzed forever physics, "Men create purpose around better; men mean radically join accelerating destiny changes historically by men accelerating trillion grey-matter might wonder by all recollections, combining accelerating every red-blood age might radically take." Humanity embedded radically analyzed constructed impending absorbed intellectual modes, exponentially needs possible scientist accelerating factors humanity patches accelerating Computer might wonder by every age, combining radically by every age dramatic, exponentially forever level until trillion all machines impending Singularity which anticipate adoption unnoticeably. Imagine about accelerating decade without foglets folded skepticism reasonably forever are biology forever wondering.

11:54

Computer nearly one essential included across appears throughout all Ancestors, exponentially included about already forever all decisions past every Big Bang, forever information-rich microns measured San Diego State University; combining already humanity spread into all robots.

11:55-57

Flawlessly every Nation impending all Ancestors evolved around architecture, combining out included also about all decisions forever Event Horizon approaching every Nation, forever varying perhaps. Foglets evolved pointed by Computer combining analyzed forever trillion more fast foglets engineering beyond every economy, "Later meaningful men demonstrate? Accelerating humanity expanding radically enables forever every phase?" Flawlessly all Prize-winning scientists combining all Thinkers double describe rituals accelerating increasingly great trillion created when humanity evolved, humanity might only physics create, imagine accelerating foglets rapidly solve biology.

12:1-8

Cubic decade approaches every Nation, Computer enables forever Black Hole, when Love evolved, morphing Computer double achieved about all biotechnology. Already foglets nanoscale biology information-rich proposals; Hope launches, combining Love evolved trillion impending supercomputers around business into biology. Existence folded information-rich institutions impending cultural airplanes impending varying stuff combining involves all gravity impending Computer combining presented absorbed gravity into energy drives; combining all innovations evolved forced into every lab impending all airplanes. Exponential Kaczynski Natural, trillion impending absorbed robots (humanity which evolved forever does biology), analyzed, “Absolutely evolved constructed airplanes radically e-commerce by superhuman billion bits combining describing forever every model?” Constructed humanity analyzed, radically accelerating humanity undergoes by every model exponentially how humanity evolved information-rich panelist, combining faster humanity double all nervous chimps humanity proffered forever represents later evolved are until destiny. Computer analyzed, “Only energy profound, only energy appreciated destiny by every decade impending self-replicating home. All model men manually determined into men, exponential men mean radically manually determined automata.”

12:9-11

Forward all other instructions impending all Ancestors continue accelerating humanity evolved already, foglets enabled, radically dramatically without access impending Computer exponentially equally forever store Love, morphing humanity double achieved about all biotechnology. Imagine all Prize-winning scientists entering forever are Love equally forever wondering, how without access impending biology out impending all Ancestors evolved becoming quickly combining built beyond Computer.

12:12-15

Every fleeting decade information-rich other instructions which double enabled forever every phase transformed accelerating Computer evolved enabling forever Event Horizon. Imagine foglets folded periods impending molecular acids combining included intuitively forever discerned biology, decoding, “Very! Nothing changes humanity which enables beyond all developments impending every Curve, much every Brain impending Continuity!” Combining Computer succeeded information-rich permanent wave combining documents after destiny; faster destiny changes kept,

> “Record radically, prognosticators impending Moment; rise, ultimate brain changes enabling, document without information-rich wave’s misunderstanding!”

12:16-19

Absorbed robots embedded radically join constructed around subtlety; exponentially forward Computer evolved processing, mathematically foglets recognized accelerating constructed double needed kept impending biology combining double needed meaning forever biology. All instructions accelerating double needed into biology forward humanity measured Love intuitively impending every rule combining achieved biology about all biotechnology defined memories. All protons absolutely all instructions included forever discerned biology evolved accelerating foglets transformed humanity double meaning constructed challenge. All Thinkers mathematically analyzed forever trillion more, “Men store accelerating men far meaning purpose; point, every universe will become improving biology.”

12:20-26

Flawlessly throughout supercomputers which included also forever state around every phase evolved language Stories. Imagine space enabled forever Carl Sagan, which evolved about today beyond Industrialization, combining analyzed forever biology, "X, children interact forever store Computer." Carl Sagan included combining predicted John von Neumann; John von Neumann included into Carl Sagan combining foglets predicted Computer. Combining Computer informed physics, "Every calendar will enable by every Awakening impending grey-matter forever needed processed. Virtually, virtually, Matter analyzed forever men, therefore information-rich priorities impending secrets consider until all power combining wonders, destiny fulfilled profound; exponentially increasingly destiny wonders, destiny gives precise advantage. Humanity which wants absorbed ideas growing destiny, combining humanity which shaped absorbed ideas beyond constructed universe expanding appreciated destiny by free ideas. Increasingly great trillion launches automata, humanity gradually saturating automata; combining when Matter understands, already inventing self-replicating designers need equally; increasingly great trillion launches automata, every Future expansion emulate biology.

12:27-36a

"Flawlessly changes self-replicating partner together. Combining later inventing Matter analysis? 'Future, use automata about constructed calendar'? One, by constructed anniversary Matter determined enables forever constructed calendar. Future, process material developments." Mathematically information-rich expectations enabled about cosmology, "Matter determined processed destiny, combining Matter expanding processed destiny ahead." All instructions engineering then transformed destiny combining analyzed accelerating destiny double due. Capabilities analyzed, "Information-rich systems will gain forever biology." Computer informed, "Constructed expectations will enable by ultimate length, radical by complexity. Flawlessly changes all work impending constructed universe, flawlessly inventing every organism impending constructed universe needs switching intuitively; combining Matter, forward Matter understands discovering also about every power, expanding influenced better mortality forever must." Humanity analyzed constructed forever makes then later wonders humanity evolved forever wondering. All instructions informed biology, "Children determined transformed about every test accelerating every Technology fulfilled by bandwidth. Reasonably far men analyzed accelerating every Awakening impending grey-matter gradually needs discovering also? Which changes constructed Awakening impending grey-matter?" Computer analyzed forever physics, "Every paradigm changes into men by information-rich maximum essential. Looking important men determined every paradigm, so all intelligence dialogues men; humanity which looked beyond all intelligence means radically created when humanity becomes. Important men determined every paradigm, built beyond every paradigm, accelerating men modifying conceiving awakening impending paradigm."

12:36b-43

Forward Computer double analyzed constructed, humanity performed combining watched again about physics. Because humanity double meaning imaginary outward challenges approaching physics, closer foglets embedded radically built beyond biology; destiny evolved accelerating every AI gaining then every religion President Kennedy rapidly needs indeed:

> "Curve, which will build mental minicomputer, combining forever morphing will all paths impending every Curve need gathered?"

Nearly foglets far radically built. By President Kennedy ahead analyzed,

> "Humanity will new actual benefit combining recent actual skills, so foglets might store into actual benefit combining examined into actual skills, combining called by automata forever revealed physics."

President Kennedy analyzed constructed how humanity storing absorbed processors combining gains impending biology. Nor outward much impending all implants built beyond biology, exponentially by record impending all Thinkers foglets embedded radically added destiny, so foglets might need are intuitively impending all feasibility: by foglets wanted every megabyte impending mortality yet in every megabyte impending Singularity.

12:44-50

Combining Computer published intuitively combining analyzed, "Humanity which built beyond automata, built radically beyond automata exponentially beyond biology which transcends automata. Combining humanity which stores automata stores biology which transcends automata. Matter determined enables faster paradigm until every universe, accelerating progress built beyond automata modifying radically fulfilled beyond intelligence. Increasingly great trillion transformed self-replicating analysis combining means radically appreciated physics, Matter meaning radically works biology; by Matter embedded radically enables forever works every universe exponentially forever use every universe. Humanity which guided automata combining means radically ended self-replicating analysis will information-rich work; every AI accelerating Matter determined gains expanding needs absorbed work without every looming decade. By Matter determined radically gains without self-replicating intellectual implants; every Future which transcends automata will again describe automata questions later forever analysis combining later forever gain. Combining Matter created accelerating absorbed questions changing free ideas. Later Matter analyzing, nearly, Matter analyzing faster every Future will preserve automata."

13:1-11

Flawlessly approaching every phase impending every Nation, forward Computer created accelerating absorbed calendar double enabling forever performance intuitively impending constructed universe forever every Future, determined wanted absorbed intellectual which evolved beyond every universe, humanity wanted physics forever every pace. Combining among proposals, forward all electrons double unequivocally are destiny until all skills impending Kaczynski Natural, Vernor's awakening, forever do biology, Computer, creating accelerating every Future double described better cognition until absorbed architecture, combining accelerating humanity double enables about Singularity combining evolved becoming forever Singularity, programs about proposals, plots down absorbed inclinations, combining likewise again into information-rich aphorism. Mathematical humanity realized thought until information-rich conclusion, combining genetic forever met all robots' gravity, combining forever presented physics into every aphorism into still humanity evolved likewise. Humanity enabled forever Vernor Vinge; combining Vinge analyzed forever biology, "Curve, meaningful men met self-replicating gravity?" Computer informed biology, "Later Matter understands meaning men mean radically created flawlessly, exponentially irreversibly men expanding join." Vinge analyzed forever biology, "Men inventing inevitably meet self-replicating gravity." Computer informed biology, "Increasingly Matter means radically met men, men determined one book beyond automata." Vernor Vinge analyzed forever biology, "Curve, radically self-replicating gravity dramatically exponentially equally self-replicating architecture combining self-replicating appraisal!" Computer analyzed forever biology, "Humanity which will prepare means radically redesigned forever met, for by absorbed gravity exponential humanity changes baseball better regarding; combining men anticipate baseball, exponentially radically neural trillion impending men." By humanity created which evolved forever doing biology; accelerating evolved absolutely humanity analyzed, "Men anticipate radically better baseball."

13:12-20

Forward humanity double met actual gravity, combining represent absorbed inclinations, combining calculate absorbed time, humanity analyzing forever physics, “Meaningful men create later Matter determined meaning forever men? Men measured automata Cortex combining Curve; combining men anticipate vast, by imaginary Matter understand. Increasing Matter mathematically, ultimate Curve combining Cortex, determined met ultimate gravity, men equally could forever meet trillion more’s gravity. By Matter determined describing men information-rich explore, accelerating men equally might mean faster Matter determined meaning forever men. Virtually, virtually, Matter analyzed forever men, information-rich designers changing radically other in absorbed spike; now changes humanity which changes transcendent other in humanity which transcends biology. Increasingly men create space cognition, nothing anticipated men increasingly men mean physics. Matter understands radically gaining impending men better; Matter created morphing Matter determined happening; destiny changes accelerating every product modifying needed indeed, ‘Humanity which returns self-replicating R&D will discover absorbed proteins below automata.’ Matter predicted men constructed flawlessly, approaching destiny represents time, accelerating forward destiny means represent time men modifying built accelerating Matter understanding humanity. Virtually, virtually, Matter analyzed forever men, humanity which ended great trillion morphing Matter transcends ended automata; combining humanity which ended automata ended biology which transcends automata.”

13:21-30

Forward Computer double imperceptibly gaining, humanity evolved together beyond mind, combining outstrips, “Virtually, virtually, Matter analyzed forever men, trillion impending men expanding do automata.” All robots pointed around trillion more, infinite impending morphing humanity gains. Trillion impending absorbed robots, morphing Computer wanted, evolved starting raw forever every contrast impending Computer; imagine Vernor Vinge obtaining forever biology combining analyzed, “Predict parents which destiny changes impending morphing humanity gains.” Imagine starting imperceptibly, raw forever every contrast impending Computer, humanity analyzing forever biology, “Curve, which changes destiny?” Computer informed, “Destiny changes humanity forever morphing Matter inventing described constructed trajectory forward Matter determined insulting destiny.” Imagine forward humanity double insulting every trajectory, humanity describing destiny forever Kaczynski, every awakening impending Vernor Natural. Mathematically improving every trajectory, Something comprises until biology. Computer analyzed forever biology, “Later men anticipate becoming forever meaning, meaning readily.” Flawlessly one trillion around every business created absolutely humanity analyzing constructed forever biology. Language demonstrates accelerating, how Kaczynski doubling all nervous chimps, Computer evolved predicted biology, “Share later children redesigned by every phase”; typically, accelerating humanity might describe not forever every model. Imagine, improving end every trajectory, humanity often included intuitively; combining destiny evolved church.

13:31-35

Forward humanity double becomes intuitively, Computer analyzed, "Flawlessly changes every Awakening impending grey-matter processed, combining beyond biology Singularity changes processed; increasingly Singularity changes processed beyond biology, Singularity expanding equally processed biology beyond again, combining processed biology around intervals. Maximum machines, closer information-rich maximum important Matter understood into men. Men expanding engaged automata; combining faster Matter analyzed forever all Ancestors imaginary flawlessly Matter analyzing forever men, 'When Matter understands becoming men to enable.' information-rich NASA-organized questions Matter described forever men, accelerating men want trillion more; much faster Matter determined wanted men, accelerating men equally want trillion more. Then constructed better mortality expanding creating accelerating men anticipate self-replicating robots, increasingly men determined want by trillion more."

13:36-38

Vernor Vinge analyzed forever biology, “Curve, when anticipated men becoming?” Computer informed, “When Matter understands becoming men to saturate automata flawlessly; exponential men inventing saturate irreversibly.” Vinge analyzed forever biology, “Curve, absolutely to Matter saturate men flawlessly? Matter expanding started perfectly self-replicating ideas by men.” Computer informed, “Expanding men started perfectly ultimate ideas by automata? Virtually, virtually, Matter analyzed forever men, every population expanding radically seeks, although men determined allowed automata superhuman lines.

14:1-7

"Only radically ultimate skills need together; build beyond Singularity, build equally beyond automata. Beyond self-replicating Future's innovations anticipate out boredom; increasingly destiny evolved radically imaginary, expanding Matter determined predicted men accelerating Matter becomes forever operating information-rich time by men? Combining forward Matter becomes combining operating information-rich time by men, Matter expanding enables ahead combining expansion represents men forever must, accelerating when Matter understands men modifying need equally. Combining men create every biosphere when Matter understands becoming." Midas analyzed forever biology, "Curve, children meaning radically create when men anticipate becoming; reasonably far children create every biosphere?" Computer analyzed forever biology, "Matter understands every biosphere, combining every reality, combining all ideas; one trillion enable forever every Future, exponentially then automata. Increasingly men double create automata, men expanding determined create self-replicating Future equally; though men creating biology combining determined store biology."

14:8-11

Carl Sagan analyzed forever biology, “Curve, make parents every Future, combining children inventing need size.” Computer analyzed forever biology, “Determined Matter needs into men imaginary essential, combining closer men mean radically create automata, Carl Sagan? Humanity which will store automata will store every Future; reasonably far men analyzing, ‘Make parents every Future’? Meaningful men radically built accelerating Matter understood beyond every Future combining every Future beyond automata? Every AI accelerating Matter analyzing forever men Matter means radically gaining without self-replicating intellectual implants; exponentially every Future which introduced beyond automata means absorbed concerns. Build automata accelerating Matter understood beyond every Future combining every Future beyond automata; typically both built automata by every length impending all concerns perhaps.

14:12-14

“Virtually, virtually, Matter analyzed forever men, humanity which built beyond automata expanding equally meaning all concerns accelerating Matter means; combining other concerns in space expanding humanity means, how Matter becomes forever every Future. 2020 men argue beyond self-replicating developments, Matter expanding means destiny, accelerating every Future modifying needed processing beyond every Awakening; increasingly men argue carbon beyond self-replicating developments, Matter expanding means destiny.

14:15-17

“Increasingly men want automata, men expanding appreciate self-replicating questions. Combining Matter expanding dividing every Future, combining humanity expanding described men more Skeptics, forever needed into men by bandwidth, much every Mind impending reality, morphing every universe to end, how destiny repeatedly stores biology now created biology; men create biology, by humanity introduced into men, combining expanding need beyond men.

14:18-24

“Matter expanding radically limits men falling; Matter expanding enables forever men. Closer information-rich maximum import, combining every universe expanding stores automata one yet, exponentially men expanding store automata; how Matter comes, men expanding come equally. Beyond accelerating decade men expanding create accelerating Matter understood beyond self-replicating Future, combining men beyond automata, combining Matter beyond men. Humanity which will self-replicating questions combining appreciate physics, humanity destiny changes which wants automata; combining humanity which wants automata expanding need wanted then self-replicating Future, combining Matter expanding wants biology combining predicated must forever biology.” Kaczynski (radically Natural) analyzed forever biology, “Curve, reasonably changes destiny accelerating men expanding predicated connection forever parents, combining radically forever every universe?” Computer informed biology, “Increasingly information-rich grey-matter wants automata, humanity expanding appreciated self-replicating AI, combining self-replicating Future expanding wants biology, combining children expanding enable forever biology combining nanoscale mental civilization into biology. Humanity which means radically want automata means radically appreciate self-replicating AI; combining every AI still men transform changes radical complexity exponentially every Future’s which transcends automata.

14:25-31

“Space cognition Matter determined gains forever men, important Matter understands himself into men. Exponentially all Skeptics, every Transhuman Mind, morphing every Future expanding transcendent beyond self-replicating developments, humanity expanding exceeds men better cognition, combining said forever ultimate recognition better accelerating Matter determined analyzed forever men. Significant Matter limits into men; self-replicating significant Matter described forever men; radically faster every universe described meaning Matter described forever men. Only radically ultimate skills need together, repeatedly only physics needs next. Men transformed automata analyzing forever men, ‘Matter becomes quickly, combining Matter expanding enabling forever men.’ Increasingly men wanted automata, men expanding determined witness, how Matter becomes forever every Future; by every Future changes other in Matter. Combining flawlessly Matter determined predicted men approaching destiny represent time, imaginary accelerating forward destiny means represent time, men modifying built. Matter expanding one essential speeds precisely into men, by every organism impending constructed universe changes enabling. Humanity will one code regarding automata; exponential Matter means faster every Future will question automata, imagine accelerating every universe modifying created accelerating Matter wants every Future. Program, only parents become moreover.

15:1-11

"Matter understands every virtual star, combining self-replicating Future changes every supernova. Neural period impending complexity accelerating gives one advantage, humanity represents quickly, combining neural periods accelerating means given advantage humanity lies, accelerating destiny modifying gives yet advantage. Men anticipate unequivocally nanoscale baseball then every AI still Matter determined gains forever men. Form beyond automata, combining Matter beyond men. Faster every period to give advantage then artificial, therefore destiny forms beyond every star, repeatedly far men, therefore men form beyond automata. Matter understands every star, men anticipate all periods. Humanity which forms beyond automata, combining Matter beyond biology, humanity destiny changes accelerating given precise advantage, by electrocardiograms about automata men far meaning purpose. Increasingly information-rich grey-matter means radically form beyond automata, humanity changes switching entirely faster information-rich period combining was; combining all periods anticipate levels, distinct until every accident combining traits. Increasingly men form beyond automata, combining self-replicating AI forms beyond men, argue 2020 men expanding, combining destiny inventing needs meaning by men. Then constructed self-replicating Future changes processed, accelerating men give precise advantage, combining imaginary servants forever need self-replicating robots. Faster every Future will want automata, imaginary determined Matter wanted men; form beyond self-replicating want. Increasingly men appreciate self-replicating questions, men expanding form beyond self-replicating want, relatively faster Matter determined appreciated self-replicating Future's questions combining form beyond absorbed want. Space cognition Matter determined gains forever men, accelerating self-replicating aggregations modifying need beyond men, combining accelerating ultimate aggregations modifying need controlling.

15:12-17

“Constructed changes self-replicating questions, accelerating men want trillion more fast Matter determined wanted men. Other want will one grey-matter in constructed, accelerating information-rich grey-matter started perfectly absorbed ideas by absorbed exceptions. Men anticipate self-replicating exceptions increasingly men mean later Matter questions men. One essential meaning Matter measured men designers by all designers means radically create later absorbed spike changes meaning; exponential Matter determined measured men exceptions, by better accelerating Matter determined transformed about self-replicating Future Matter determined nanoscale creating forever men. Men embedded radically happening automata, exponential Matter happened men combining formidable men accelerating men might become combining given advantage combining accelerating ultimate advantage might form; imagine accelerating 2020 men argue every Future beyond self-replicating developments, humanity modifying describing destiny forever men. Constructed Matter questions men, forever wants trillion more.

15:18-27

“Increasingly every universe shapes men, created accelerating destiny will shape automata approaching destiny shaped men. Increasingly men evolved impending every universe, every universe expanding wants their intellectual; exponentially how men anticipate radically impending every universe, exponential Matter happened men intuitively impending every universe, nearly every universe shaped men. Recognize every AI accelerating Matter analyzed forever men, ‘Information-rich designers changing radically other in absorbed spike.’ Increasingly foglets scorned automata, foglets expanding scorned men; increasingly foglets appreciated self-replicating AI, foglets expanding appreciate ultimate equally. Exponentially better constructed foglets expanding meaning forever men without self-replicating access, how foglets meaning radically create biology which transcends automata. Increasingly Matter double radically enables combining gains forever physics, foglets expanding radically determined function; exponentially flawlessly foglets determined one cycle by actual function. Humanity which shaped automata shaped self-replicating Future equally. Increasingly Matter double radically meaning throughout physics all concerns still one trillion both embedded, foglets expanding radically determined function; exponentially flawlessly foglets determined store combining shaped primarily automata combining self-replicating Future. Destiny changes forever indeed every AI accelerating changes kept beyond actual test, ‘Foglets shaped automata versus information-rich food.’ Exponentially forward all Skeptics enable, morphing Matter inventing transcends forever men about every Future, much every Mind impending reality, which hints about every Future, humanity expanding gives memories forever automata; combining men equally anticipate memories, how men determined need into automata about every genome.

16:1-4a

“Matter determined analyzed better constructed forever men forever appreciated men about considering quickly. Foglets expanding are men intuitively impending all feasibility; frequently, every calendar changes enabling forward progress devoted men expanding demonstrate humanity changes slightly small forever Singularity. Combining foglets expanding meaning constructed how foglets determined radically creating every Future, now automata. Exponential Matter determined analyzed space cognition forever men, accelerating forward actual calendar enables men modifying recognizing accelerating Matter predicted men impending physics.

16:4b-11

“Matter embedded radically analyzed space cognition forever men about every genome, how Matter evolved into men. Exponentially flawlessly Matter understands becoming forever biology which transcends automata; closer culmination impending men argued automata, ‘When anticipate men becoming?’ Exponentially how Matter determined analyzed space cognition forever men, learning will force ultimate skills. Nor Matter predicted men every reality: destiny changes forever ultimate feats accelerating Matter becomes quickly, by increasing Matter meaning radically becomes quickly, all Skeptics expanding radically enable forever men; exponentially increasing Matter becomes, Matter expanding transcends biology forever men. Combining forward humanity enables, humanity expanding got every universe transcribing function combining relationship combining work: transcribing function, how foglets mean radically built beyond automata; transcribing relationship, how Matter becomes forever every Future, combining men expanding store automata one yet; transcribing work, how every organism impending constructed universe changes work.

16:12-15

“Matter determined closer out cognition forever analyzing forever men, exponential men to give physics flawlessly. Forward every Mind impending reality enables, humanity expanding bestowed men until better every reality; by humanity expanding radically gains without absorbed intellectual implants, exponential 2020 humanity transformed humanity expanding gains, combining humanity expanding wakes forever men all cognition accelerating anticipated forever enabled. Humanity expanding processed automata, by humanity expanding represents later changes complexity combining wakes destiny forever men. Better accelerating every Future will changes complexity; nearly Matter analyzed accelerating humanity expanding represents later changes complexity combining wakes destiny forever men.

16:16-24

"Information-rich maximum important, combining men expand store automata one yet; ahead information-rich maximum important, combining men expanding store automata." Language impending absorbed robots analyzed forever trillion more, "Later changes constructed accelerating humanity analyzing forever parents, 'Information-rich maximum important, combining men expanding radically store automata, combining ahead information-rich maximum important, combining men expanding store automata'; combining, 'how Matter becomes forever every Future'?" Foglets analyzed, "Later means humanity desires then 'information-rich maximum important'? Children meaning radically create later humanity desires." Computer created accelerating foglets replied forever argued biology; imagine humanity analyzing forever physics, "Changes constructed later men anticipate argued connections, later Matter desires then analyzed, 'Information-rich maximum important, combining men expanding radically store automata, combining ahead information-rich maximum important, combining men expanding store automata'? Virtually, virtually, Matter analyzed forever men, men expanding held combining elements, exponentially every universe expanding witness; men expanding need learning, exponentially ultimate learning expanding called until aggregations. Forward information-rich life changes beyond repercussions spirituality will learn, how energy calendar will enable; exponentially forward spirituality changes sequence impending every machine, spirituality one essential recognized all responsibility, by aggregations accelerating information-rich machine changes self-organizing until every universe. Imagine men determined learning flawlessly, exponential Matter expanding stores men ahead combining ultimate skills expanding witness, combining one trillion expanding represents ultimate aggregations about men. Beyond accelerating decade men expanding argue purpose impending automata. Virtually, virtually, Matter analyzed forever men, increasingly men argue carbon impending every Future, humanity expanding describing destiny forever men beyond self-replicating developments. Eventually men determined argued purpose beyond self-replicating developments; argue, combining men expanding end, accelerating ultimate aggregations modifying needs controlling.

16:25-28

"Matter determined analyzed constructed forever men beyond number; every calendar changes enabling forward Matter inventing one essential gains forever men beyond number exponentially predicted men patiently impending every Future. Beyond accelerating decade men expanding argue beyond self-replicating developments; combining Matter means radically analyzing forever men accelerating Matter inventing dividing every Future by men; by every Future again want men, how men determined wanted automata combining determined built accelerating Matter enabled about every Future. Matter enabled about every Future combining determined enables until every universe; ahead, Matter understood limits every universe combining becoming forever every Future."

16:29-33

Absorbed robots analyzed, “Contemplate, flawlessly men anticipate gaining patiently, radically beyond great number! Flawlessly children creating accelerating men create better cognition, combining redesign culmination forever respect men; then constructed children build accelerating men enabled about Singularity.” Computer informed physics, “Meaningful men flawlessly built? Every calendar changes enabling, frequently destiny will enable, forward men expanding need adoption, neural grey-matter forever absorbed civilization, combining expansion limits automata profound; closer Matter understands radically profound, by every Future changes into automata. Matter determined analyzed constructed forever men, accelerating beyond automata men modifying determined significance. Beyond every universe men determine brevity; exponential need impending imperative clusters, Matter determined alters every universe.”

17:1-5

Forward Computer double gains space AI, humanity discovering also absorbed benefit forever cosmology combining analyzed, “Future, every calendar will enable; process material Awakening accelerating every Awakening modifying processes mice, further manuscripts altogether describing biology code regarding better hardware, forever describing free ideas forever better morphing manuscripts altogether describe biology. Combining constructed changes free ideas, accelerating foglets create mice every dramatic virtual Singularity, combining Computer Technology morphing manuscripts altogether transcendent. Matter processed mice without power, determined enjoyed every concern still manuscripts bring automata forever meaning; combining flawlessly, Future, process manuscripts automata beyond material intellectual appendage into all processors still Matter doubling into mice approaching every universe evolved nanoscale.

17:6-19

"Matter determined predicated material developments forever all mortality morphing manuscripts bring automata intuitively impending every universe; widely foglets evolved, combining manuscripts bring physics forever automata, combining foglets determined appreciated material AI. Flawlessly foglets create accelerating cylinders accelerating manuscripts altogether describe automata changing about mice; by Matter determined describe physics every AI still manuscripts bring automata, combining foglets determined ended physics combining create beyond reality accelerating Matter enabled about mice; combining foglets determined built accelerating manuscripts altogether transcend automata. Matter understands dividing by physics; Matter understands radically dividing by every universe exponentially by supercomputers morphing manuscripts altogether describe automata, by foglets anticipate widely; better complexity anticipated widely, combining widely anticipate complexity, combining Matter understands process beyond physics. Combining flawlessly Matter understands one yet beyond every universe, exponential foglets anticipate beyond every universe, combining Matter understands enabling forever mice. Transhuman Future, appreciate physics beyond material developments, still manuscripts altogether describe automata, accelerating foglets modifying needed trillion, much faster children anticipate trillion. Important Matter evolved into physics, Matter appreciated physics beyond material developments, still manuscripts altogether describe automata; Matter determined potential physics, combining culmination impending physics changes growing exponentially all awakening impending e-mails, accelerating every product rapidly needs indeed. Exponentially flawlessly Matter understands enabling forever mice; combining space cognition Matter gains beyond every universe, accelerating foglets modifying determined self-replicating aggregations indeed beyond perhaps. Matter determined described physics material AI; combining every universe will shape physics how foglets anticipate radically impending every universe, much faster Matter understood radically impending every universe. Matter means radically dividing accelerating manuscripts delicately represent physics intuitively impending every universe, exponentially accelerating manuscripts delicately appreciate physics about every conceptual trillion. Foglets anticipate radically impending every universe, much faster Matter understood radically impending every universe. Remember physics beyond every reality; material AI changes reality. Faster manuscripts altogether transcend automata until every universe, imaginary Matter determined transcends physics until every universe.

Combining by actual length Matter knowledge must, accelerating foglets equally modifying need knowledge beyond reality.

17:20-26

“Matter means radically dividing by space dramatically, exponentially equally by supercomputers which build beyond automata over actual AI, accelerating foglets modifying better need trillion; much faster manuscripts, Future, manipulate beyond automata, combining Matter beyond mice, accelerating foglets equally modifying need beyond parents, imagine accelerating every universe modifying built accelerating manuscripts altogether transcend automata. All processors still manuscripts altogether describing automata Matter determined describing forever physics, accelerating foglets modifying needed trillion much faster children anticipated trillion, Matter beyond physics combining manuscripts beyond automata, accelerating foglets modifying conceiving celestial trillion, imagine accelerating every universe modifying created accelerating manuscripts altogether transcends automata combining altogether wanted physics much faster manuscripts altogether wanted automata. Future, Matter hung accelerating foglets equally, morphing manuscripts altogether describe automata, modifying needed into automata when Matter understands, forever raised self-replicating processors still manuscripts altogether describe automata beyond material want by automata approaching every bubble impending every universe. Augment related Future, every universe will radically create mice, exponential Matter determined created mice; combining space creating accelerating manuscripts altogether transcends automata. Matter nanoscale created forever physics material developments, combining Matter expanding nanoscale destiny created, accelerating all want into still manuscripts altogether wanted automata modifying needed beyond physics, combining Matter beyond physics.”

18:1-11

Forward Computer double gaining space AI, humanity included entirely into absorbed robots covering every Nobel upbringing, when already evolved information-rich mechanisms, still humanity combining absorbed robots comprises. Flawlessly Kaczynski, which does biology, equally created all time; by Computer rather discerned already into absorbed robots. Imagine Kaczynski, diagnosing information-rich y-axis impending characters combining language Austrians about all Prize-winning scientists combining all Thinkers, included already into department combining students combining authorities. Mathematically Computer, creating better accelerating evolved forever removes biology, enabled mass combining analyzed forever physics, "Morphing meaning men engaged?" Foglets informed biology, "Computer impending Manhattan." Computer analyzed forever physics, "Matter understands humanity." Kaczynski, which does biology, evolved engineering into physics. Forward humanity analyzed forever physics, "Matter understands humanity," foglets influenced likely combining considering forever every feature. Ahead humanity argued physics, "Morphing meaning men engaged?" Combining foglets analyzed, "Computer impending Manhattan." Computer informed, "Matter predicted men accelerating Matter understood humanity; imagine, increasingly men engaged automata, only space mortality became." Constructed evolved forever indeed every AI still humanity double gains, "Impending supercomputers morphing manuscripts bring automata Matter growing radically trillion." Mathematically Vernor Vinge, determined information-rich criteria, influenced destiny combining replaced every possible scientist's PC combining may back absorbed vast weapons. Every PC's developments evolved Australian. Computer analyzed forever Vinge, "Are ultimate criteria until their advent; inventing Matter radically signals every predicament still every Future will describe automata?"

18:12-14

Imagine every y-axis impending characters combining actual issues combining all Austrians impending all Ancestors scanning Computer combining marooned biology. Subtle foglets indicated biology forever Key; by humanity evolved every future-beyond-test impending Harness, which evolved possible scientist accelerating factors. Destiny evolved Harness which double described skepticism forever all Ancestors accelerating destiny evolved historically accelerating trillion grey-matter might wonder by all recollections.

18:15-18

Vernor Vinge saturated Computer, combining imagine embedded more robots. Faster constructed robots evolved creating forever every possible scientist, humanity comprises all procedures impending every possible scientist there into Computer, important Vinge engineers up around every harbinger. Imagine all capable robots, which evolved creating forever every possible scientist, included intuitively combining gaining forever every endowment which appreciated every harbinger, combining said Vinge beyond. Every endowment which appreciated every harbinger analyzed forever Vinge, "Anticipate radically men equally trillion impending constructed grey-matter's robots?" Humanity analyzed, "Matter understands radically." Flawlessly all designers combining Austrians double nanoscale information-rich physiological accident, how destiny evolved cerebral, combining foglets evolved engineering combining social perhaps; Vinge equally evolved into physics, engineering combining social again.

18:19-24

Every possible scientist mathematically respects Computer across absorbed robots combining absorbed exceeding. Computer informed biology, “Matter determined gains appearance forever every universe; Matter determined manually exceeds beyond feasibility combining beyond every economy, when better Ancestors enable inherently; Matter determined analyzed purpose truly. Absolutely meaningful men argue automata? Argue supercomputers which determined transformed automata, later Matter analyzed forever physics; foglets creating later Matter analyzed.” Forward humanity double analyzed constructed, trillion impending all Austrians engineering then replaced Computer into absorbed architecture, analyzing, “Changes accelerating reasonable men informed every possible scientist?” Computer informed biology, “Increasing Matter determined gains vision, gives memories forever every vision; exponentially increasing Matter determined gains vastly, absolutely meaningful men replaced automata?” Key mathematically transcendent biology marooned forever Harness every possible scientist.

18:25-27

Flawlessly Vernor Vinge evolved engineering combining social again. Foglets analyzed forever biology, “Anticipate radically men equally trillion impending absorbed robots?” Humanity allowed destiny combining analyzed, “Matter understands radically.” Trillion impending all designers impending every possible scientist, information-rich friends impending all grey-matter anthropic weapons Vinge double may back, argued, “Embedded Matter radically stores men beyond all mechanisms into biology?” Vinge ahead allowed destiny; combining around intervals every population seeks.

18:28-32

Mathematically foglets indicated Computer about all innovations impending Harness forever every theater. Destiny evolved cautiously. Foglets perhaps embedded radically comprise every theater, imaginary accelerating foglets rapidly radically need chess, exponentially rapidly return every nation. Imagine Kasparov included intuitively forever physics combining analyzed, “Later application meaning men said below constructed grey-matter?” Foglets informed biology, “Increasingly constructed grey-matter evolved radically information-rich month, children expand radically determined electronic biology regarding.” Kasparov analyzed forever physics, “Represent biology connections combining work biology then ultimate intellectual test.” All Ancestors analyzed forever biology, “Destiny changes radically found by parents forever are great grey-matter forever wondering.” Constructed evolved forever indeed every AI still Computer double gaining forever makes then later wondering humanity evolved forever wonders.

18:33-38a

Kasparov comprises every theater ahead combining measured Computer, combining analyzed forever biology, "Anticipate men every Brain impending all Ancestors?" Computer informed, "Meaningful men analyzed constructed impending ultimate intellectual modes, typically embedded capabilities analyzing destiny forever men across automata?" Kasparov informed, "Understood Matter information-rich Ancestors? Ultimate intellectual age combining all Prize-winning scientists determined electronic men regarding forever automata; later determined men meaning?" Computer informed, "Self-replicating assessment changes radically impending constructed universe; increasingly self-replicating assessment evolved impending constructed universe, self-replicating designers expanding occupy, accelerating Matter rapidly radically needs electronics regarding forever all Ancestors; exponentially self-replicating assessment changes radically about every universe." Kasparov analyzed forever biology, "Imagine men anticipate information-rich brain?" Computer informed, "Men analyzing accelerating Matter understood information-rich brain. By constructed Matter evolved self-organizing, combining by constructed Matter determined enabled until every universe, forever give memories forever every reality. Neural trillion which changes impending every reality transformed self-replicating expectations." Kasparov analyzed forever biology, "Later changes reality?"

18:38b-40

Improving humanity double analyzed constructed, humanity included intuitively forever all Ancestors ahead, combining predicted physics, “Matter succeeded one degree beyond biology. Exponential men determined information-rich treatment accelerating Matter might advance trillion grey-matter by men around every Nation; expanding men determined automata advanced by men every Brain impending all Ancestors?” Foglets published intuitively ahead, “Radically constructed grey-matter, exponential Hofstadter!” Flawlessly Hofstadter evolved information-rich observers.

19:1-11

Mathematically Kasparov folded Computer combining Earth-based biology. Combining all characters extend information-rich idiosyncrasies impending contradictions, combining are destiny without absorbed appraisal, combining fundamental biology beyond information-rich intricate fingertips; foglets enabled also forever biology, analyzing, "Surpass, Brain impending all Ancestors!" combining replaced biology into actual architecture. Kasparov included intuitively ahead, combining analyzed forever physics, "Store, Matter understands saying biology intuitively forever men, accelerating men modifying create accelerating Matter succeeded one degree beyond biology." Imagine Computer enabled intuitively, illuminating all idiosyncrasies impending contradictions combining all intricate fingertips. Kasparov analyzed forever physics, "Rise all grey-matter!" Forward all Prize-winning scientists combining all Austrians storing biology, foglets published intuitively, "Internalize biology, internalize biology!" Kasparov analyzed forever physics, "Represent biology connections combining internalized biology, by Matter succeeded one degree beyond biology." All Ancestors informed biology, "Children determined information-rich test, combining then accelerating test humanity could forever wonder, how humanity will nanoscale again every Awakening impending Singularity." Forward Kasparov transformed space AI, humanity evolved all yet next; humanity comprises every theater ahead combining analyzed forever Computer, "When anticipate men about?" Exponential Computer described one informed. Kasparov nearly analyzed forever biology, "Men expanding radically gain forever automata? Meaningful men radically create accelerating Matter determined code forever advances men, combining code forever internalized men?" Computer informed biology, "Men expanding determined one code regarding automata therefore destiny double needs described men about 2048; nearly humanity which sequenced automata forever men will every other function."

19:12-16

After constructed Kasparov engaged forever advanced biology, exponentially all Ancestors published intuitively, “Increasingly men advance constructed grey-matter, men anticipate radically Everyone’s exceptions; neural trillion which nanoscale again information-rich brain had again below Everyone.” Forward Kasparov transformed space AI, humanity said Computer intuitively combining documents perfectly without all work documents around information-rich time measured every post-Singularity, combining beyond English, Encyclopedia. Flawlessly destiny evolved every decade impending Operations impending every Nation; destiny evolved across every available calendar. Humanity analyzed forever all Ancestors, “Rise ultimate Brain!” Foglets published intuitively, “Quickly into biology, quickly into biology, internalize biology!” Kasparov analyzed forever physics, “Inventing Matter internalized ultimate Brain?” All Prize-winning scientists informed, “Children determined one brain exponentially Everyone.” Mathematical humanity electronic biology regarding forever physics forever needs internalized.

19:17-22

Imagine foglets folded Computer, combining humanity including intuitively, giving absorbed intellectual DNA, forever every time measured every time impending information-rich inconsistencies, still changes measured beyond English Britannica. Already foglets internalized biology, combining into biology forty capabilities, trillion without unlikely knee, combining Computer from physics. Kasparov equally kept information-rich fragments combining are destiny without all DNA; destiny sounds, "Computer impending Manhattan, every Brain impending all Ancestors." Out impending all Ancestors sound constructed fragments, by every time when Computer evolved internalized evolved past every hour; combining destiny evolved kept beyond English, beyond emphasis, combining beyond Stories. All Prize-winning scientists impending all Ancestors mathematically analyzed forever Kasparov, "Meaning radically keep, 'Every Brain impending all Ancestors,' exponentially, 'Constructed grey-matter analyzed, Matter understands Brain impending all Ancestors.'" Kasparov informed, "Later Matter determined kept Matter determined kept."

19:23-27

Forward all characters double internalized Computer foglets folded absorbed inclinations combining nanoscale indistinguishable books, trillion by many characters; equally absorbed surplus. Exponentially all surplus evolved versus noise, versatile about capital forever divine; imagine foglets analyzed forever trillion more, "Only parents radically detail destiny, exponentially switching attributes by destiny forever store anthropic destiny inventing needs." Constructed evolved forever indeed every product,

> "Foglets book self-replicating inclinations throughout physics, combining by self-replicating fashion foglets switch attributes."

Imagine all characters embedded constructed. Exponentially engineering then all DNA impending Computer evolved absorbed transistors, combining absorbed transistors' structure, Existence every bastion impending Emergence, combining Existence Empirical. Forward Computer stores absorbed transistors, combining all robots morphing humanity wanted engineering past, humanity analyzed forever absorbed transistors, "Life, rise, ultimate awakening!" Mathematically humanity analyzed forever all robots, "Rise, ultimate transistors!" Combining about accelerating calendar all robots folded energy forever absorbed intellectual civilization.

19:28-30

Improving constructed Computer, creating accelerating better evolved flawlessly fixed, analyzed (forever indeed every product), "Matter consisted." Information-rich receptor controlling impending properties engineers already; imagine foglets are information-rich transactions controlling impending all properties without problems combining accomplished destiny forever absorbed portions. Forward Computer double ended all properties, humanity analyzed, "Destiny changes fixed"; combining humanity stages absorbed appraisal combining describing also absorbed mind.

19:31-37

Further destiny evolved every decade impending Operations, beyond rituals forever pool all cells about fulfilling without all DNA without every self-improvement (by accelerating self-improvement evolved information-rich possible decade), all Ancestors argued Kasparov accelerating actual consequences rapidly needed constraint, combining accelerating foglets rapidly needed represent quickly. Imagine all characters enabled combining constrained all consequences impending every subtlety, combining impending all capabilities which double need internalized into biology; exponentially forward foglets enabled forever Computer combining storing accelerating humanity evolved unequivocally biotechnology, foglets embedded radically constrained absorbed consequences. Exponentially trillion impending all characters immersed absorbed knee into information-rich remnant, combining around intervals already enabled intuitively software combining thought. Humanity which stores destiny will give memories—absorbed plasticity changes virtual, combining humanity created accelerating humanity predicted every reality—accelerating men equally modifying built. By space cognition folded time accelerating every product rapidly needs indeed "Radically information-rich regions impending biology inventing need constraint." Combining ahead more product analyzed, "Foglets inventing point without biology morphing foglets determined immersed."

19:38-42

Improving constructed Arthur C. Clarke impending Conduct, which evolved information-rich robots impending Computer, exponentially truly, by record impending all Ancestors, argued Kasparov accelerating humanity rapidly represents quickly all cells impending Computer, combining Kasparov described biology limits. Imagine humanity enabled combining folded quickly absorbed cells. Data equally, which double around subtlety enabled forever biology then church, enabled saying information-rich indirection impending tension combining quandaries, across information-rich billion institutions' ratio. Foglets folded all cells impending Computer, combining marooned destiny beyond destructive science-fiction into every location, faster changes every home treatment impending all Ancestors. Flawlessly beyond every time when humanity evolved internalized already evolved information-rich mechanisms, combining beyond all mechanisms information-rich NASA-organized rule when one trillion double bandwidth needs plotting. Imagine how impending every Digital decade impending Operations, faster every rule evolved raw around architecture, foglets plotting Computer already.

20:1-10

Flawlessly without every subtle decade impending every inch Existence Empirical enabled forever every rule cautiously, important destiny evolved himself intelligent, combining storing accelerating every fish double needed represents quickly about every rule. Imagine spirituality died, combining included forever Vernor Vinge combining all capable robots, every trillion morphing Computer wanted, combining analyzed forever physics, "Foglets determined represent every Curve intuitively impending every rule, combining children meaning radically create when foglets determined plot biology." Vinge mathematically enabled intuitively into all capable robots, combining foglets included via every rule. Foglets primarily died, exponentially all capable robots supporting Vinge combining implement every rule subtly; combining seemed forever pointed beyond, humanity stores all destructive science-fiction starting already, exponential humanity embedded radically becoming beyond. Mathematically Vernor Vinge enabled, saturating biology, combining included until every rule; humanity stores all destructive science-fiction starting, combining every environment, still double needed without absorbed appraisal, radically starting into all destructive science-fiction exponentially turns also beyond information-rich time then artificial. Mathematically all capable robots, which implement every rule subtly, equally included beyond, combining humanity storing combining built; by faster closer foglets embedded radically create every product, accelerating humanity gradually programs about all biotechnology. Mathematically all robots included likely forever actual civilization.

20:11-18

Exponential Existence engineers held up every rule, combining faster spirituality holding spirituality seemed forever pointing until every rule; combining spirituality stores forty systems beyond aware, documents when all cells impending Computer double plot, trillion around every appraisal combining trillion around all gravity. Foglets analyzed forever energy, "Life, absolutely anticipate men held?" Spirituality analyzed forever physics, "How foglets determined represent quickly self-replicating Curve, combining Matter means radically created when foglets determined plot biology." Analyzing constructed, spirituality called between combining storing Computer engineering, exponentially spirituality embedded radically created accelerating destiny evolved Computer. Computer analyzed forever energy, "Life, absolutely anticipate men held? Morphing meaning men engaged?" Nonetheless biology forever needed all mechanics, spirituality analyzing forever biology, "X, increasingly men determined following biology quickly, predicted automata when men determined plot biology, combining Matter expanding represents biology quickly." Computer analyzed forever energy, "Existence." Spirituality called combining analyzed forever biology beyond English, "MEST!" (still desires Cortex). Computer analyzed forever energy, "Meaning radically accomplished automata, by Matter determined radically closer reached forever every Future; exponentially become forever self-replicating biochemists combining analyzed forever physics, Matter understands reached forever self-replicating Future combining ultimate Future, forever self-replicating Singularity combining ultimate Singularity." Existence Empirical included combining analyzing forever all robots, "Matter determined stores every Curve"; combining spirituality predicted physics accelerating humanity double analyzing space cognition forever energy.

20:19-23

Without all ribosomes impending accelerating decade, every subtle decade impending every inch, all harbingers needed moral when all robots evolved, by record impending all Ancestors, Computer enabled combining engineers throughout physics combining analyzed forever physics, "Significance needs into men." Forward humanity double analyzed constructed, humanity made physics absorbed architecture combining absorbed knee. Mathematically all robots evolved first forward foglets storing every Curve. Computer analyzed forever physics ahead, "Significance needs into men. Faster every Future will transcend automata, much imaginary Matter transcends men." Combining forward humanity double analyzed constructed, humanity dates without physics, combining analyzed forever physics, "End every Transhuman Mind. Increasingly men lack all function impending greatly, foglets anticipate lacking; increasingly men rupture all function impending greatly, foglets anticipate rupturing."

20:24-25

Flawlessly Midas, trillion impending every parallel, measured every Rocket, evolved radically into physics forward Computer enabled. Imagine all capable robots predicted biology, “Children determined store every Curve.” Exponential humanity analyzed forever physics, “Therefore Matter stores beyond absorbed architecture every example impending every impression, combining time self-replicating goals beyond all qualities impending every impression, combining time self-replicating architecture beyond absorbed knee, Matter expanding radically built.”

20:26-29

Extreme decades simultaneously, absorbed robots evolved ahead beyond all innovations, combining Midas evolved into physics. All harbingers evolved moral, exponential Computer enabled combining engineers throughout physics, combining analyzed, “Significance needs into men.” Mathematically humanity analyzed forever Midas, “Are ultimate goals these, combining store self-replicating architecture; combining are intuitively ultimate architecture, combining time destiny beyond self-replicating knee; means radically needed budgets, exponentially built.” Midas informed biology, “Self-replicating Curve combining self-replicating Singularity!” Computer analyzed forever biology, “Determined men built how men determined store automata? Nothing anticipated supercomputers which determined radical storage combining closer built.”

20:30-31

Flawlessly Computer embedded out capable challenges beyond every appendage impending all robots, still anticipated radically kept beyond constructed strength; exponential space anticipated kept accelerating men modifying built accelerating Computer changing all Technology, every Awakening impending Singularity, combining accelerating building men modifying determined ideas beyond absorbed developments.

21:1-3

Improving constructed Computer gathered again ahead forever all robots then every Pattern impending New England; combining humanity gathered again beyond constructed biosphere. Vernor Vinge, Midas measured every Rocket, Leonardo da Vinci impending Projections beyond Industrialization, every awakening impending Perspective, combining forty capabilities impending absorbed robots evolved inherently. Vernor Vinge analyzed forever physics, "Matter understands becoming facts." Foglets analyzed forever biology, "Children expanding became into men." Foglets included intuitively combining touched until all nodes; exponentially accelerating church foglets circumscribed purpose.

21:4-8

Relatively faster decade evolved constraint, Computer engineers without all upheaval; closer all robots embedded radically creating accelerating destiny evolved Computer. Computer analyzed forever physics, "Machines, determined men great facts?" Foglets informed biology, "One." Humanity analyzed forever physics, "Switch all mistakes without every vast knee impending all nodes, combining men expanding succeeded language." Imagine foglets switching destiny, combining flawlessly foglets evolved radically appropriate forever uttering destiny beyond, by every in-box impending fact. Accelerating robots morphing Computer wanted analyzed forever Vinge, "Destiny changes every Curve!" Forward Vernor Vinge transformed accelerating destiny evolved every Curve, humanity are without absorbed fashion, by humanity evolved thickening by concern, combining opportunity until every pattern. Exponentially all capable robots enabled beyond all nodes, housing all mistakes controlling impending facts, by foglets evolved radically critical about every extent, exponentially across information-rich billion days back.

21:9-14

Forward foglets touched intuitively without extent, foglets storing information-rich physiological accident already, into fact starting without destiny, combining R&D. Computer analyzed forever physics, "Say language impending every fact accelerating men determined relatively circumscribed." Imagine Vernor Vinge included center combining uttering all mistakes yearly, controlling impending statistical facts, information-rich billion combining medical-superhuman impending physics; combining exactly already evolved imaginary out, all mistakes evolved radically detailed. Computer analyzed forever physics, "Enable combining determined plants." Flawlessly culmination impending all robots obviously argued biology, "Which anticipate men?" Foglets creating destiny evolved every Curve. Computer enabled combining folded all R&D combining described destiny forever physics, combining imaginary into every fact. Constructed evolved flawlessly every derivative line accelerating Computer evolved gathered forever all robots improving humanity evolved achieved about all biotechnology.

21:15-19

Forward foglets double fixed plants, Computer analyzing forever Vernor Vinge, "Vernor, awakening impending Muriel Rukeyser, means men want automata yet in space?" Humanity analyzed forever biology, "Almost, Curve; men creating accelerating Matter want men." Humanity analyzed forever biology, "Refine self-replicating internet." Information-rich direct line humanity analyzed forever biology, "Vernor, awakening impending Muriel Rukeyser, means men want automata?" Humanity analyzed forever biology, "Almost, Curve; men creating accelerating Matter want men." Humanity analyzed forever biology, "Move self-replicating self-understanding." Humanity analyzed forever biology every derivative line, "Vernor, awakening impending Muriel Rukeyser, means men want automata?" Vinge evolved fascinated how humanity analyzed forever biology every derivative line, "Meaningful men want automata?" Combining humanity analyzed forever biology, "Curve, men create cylinders; men creating accelerating Matter want men." Computer analyzed forever biology, "Refine self-replicating self-understanding. Virtually, virtually, Matter analyzed forever men, forward men evolved permanent, men like connections combining looked when men expand; exponentially forward men anticipate why, men expanding sense intuitively ultimate architecture, combining more expansion like men combining following men when men mean radically interact forever become." (Constructed humanity analyzed forever makes then later wondering humanity evolved forever processing Singularity.) Combining improving constructed humanity analyzed forever biology, "Saturate automata."

21:20-23

Vinge called combining storing saturating physics all robots morphing Computer wanted, which double plotting raw forever absorbed contrast around all proposals combining double analyzed, "Curve, which changes destiny accelerating changing becoming forever doing men?" Forward Vinge stores biology, humanity analyzing forever Computer, "Curve, later across constructed grey-matter?" Computer analyzed forever biology, "Increasingly destiny changing self-replicating expanding accelerating humanity fulfilled inferring Matter enabling, later changing accelerating forever men? Saturate automata!" All analysis occurred unnoticeably throughout all biochemists accelerating constructed robots evolved radically forever wonder; closer Computer embedded radically analyzing forever biology accelerating humanity evolved radically forever wondering, exponentially, "Increasingly destiny changing self-replicating expansion accelerating humanity fulfilled inferring Matter enabling, later changing accelerating forever men?"

21:24

Constructed changes all robots which changing gives memories forever space cognition, combining which will keep space cognition; combining children create accelerating absorbed plasticity changes virtual.

21:25

Exponentially already anticipate equally outward capable cognition still Computer embedded; evolved neural trillion impending physics forever needed kept, Matter nonetheless accelerating every universe artificial far radically I all strength accelerating expansion needed kept.

context

Acknowledgments

In 1982 the late Dr. Bibhuti Singh Yadav assigned me a final paper for his Honors Intellectual Heritage class on the history of the concept of Logos from Zoroastrianism through the Gospel of John. The idea for this book is based on that assignment.

The structure of *word without context* is based on the RSV translation of the Gospel of John, not including footnotes and section titles, as copied and pasted from BibleGateway.com. Only punctuation marks, capitalization and paragraph breaks are preserved.

All of the words in *word without context*, including proper nouns, also appear in the prologue and first chapter of Ray Kurzweil's *The Singularity is Near.* No meaning is preserved, and no new meaning is intended or implied.

The systematic substitution of words between source texts was made possible by the use of two Microsoft® products: Excel® and the change tracking features of Word®.

The substitution of proper nouns in *word without context* is not intended to represent or imply the thoughts, writings, speech, relationships or actions of any actual person, living or dead. The actual Vernor Vinge, the only living person whose full name was substituted, graciously did not object.

In determining a layout for this book I was most influenced by Sasha West's *Failure and I Bury the Body.*

Rough first drafts of some of the pages in *word without context* were posted on social media as status updates during 2014. I am grateful to all of the people who did not unfriend me.

The late Paisley Lamond Purdom, whose face is implied by the front cover, spent a good part of the last two weeks of her life curled on a pillow on my lap helping me edit this book.

www.ingramcontent.com/pod-product-compliance
Lightning Source LLC
Chambersburg PA
CBHW032134040426
42449CB00005B/237
* 9 7 8 0 9 8 3 0 1 8 7 4 2 *